SERGE

MW01282368

"**SERGEANT-AT-ARMS Bible**" is the fourth book in the *Motorcycle Club Bible* series. It is a "how-to" manual that teaches the Sergeant-at-Arms how to uphold the brotherhood's bylaws, maintain its discipline, administer its accountability system, provide security for its brothers, and fight its wars!

About the cover: The Sergeant-at-Arms shield was drawn by artist and full patch brother of the Mighty Black Sabbath MC Nation former National Business Manager Tim '*Strictly Business*' Cullen

Library of Congress Control Number: 2016919340
International Standard Book Number: 978-0-9974322-2-0

Disclaimer

The information in this book was written exclusively to provide helpful information for Sergeants-at-Arms of 99%er traditional motorcycle clubs. It does not attempt in any way to depict how Sergeants-at-Arms of 1%er motorcycle club nations should handle their duties or responsibilities. In fact 1%er subject matter is completely beyond the scope of this book and should be sought elsewhere. References in this book are provided for informational purposes only and do not constitute endorsement of any websites or other sources. Readers should be aware that the websites listed in this book may change at any time.

My Utmost to My MC

THANK YOU

To **Nashera Dominique Pitts**—you taught me to protect those whom God places in your life with everything within you; including your very life—if that's what it takes. Because failure to do so means that you fail in every category—most especially in the category of being a man.

To my Atlanta Black Sabbath MC brother **Tim Cullen**—Thanks for drawing the cover to **SERGEANT-AT-ARMS BIBLE** in just one day! You rock brother! BSFFBS

To **Christin Chapman**—Thanks for being there through thick and thin, for editing all of my books, for helping me lose 100 pounds, and for helping me survive heartbreak.

To **Jim Morgan**— Thanks for showing me how to have a small publishing empire. ☺ "Everything you need to do is everything you need to do."

To author **Larry Kollar**—Thanks for teaching me how to publish books in Create Space and Kindle, using Sigil, Scrivener and Scrapple. You didn't have to take the time but I'm so thankful that you did.

To my buddies **Bob Coleman** and **Bob Schultz**—thank you for the ears to bend and advice that never steers me wrong.

To **Marcell 'Big Cell' Tillman**—thank you for teaching me how to maximize my YouTube and FB Go Live feeds and for the opportunity on the radio show. Thanks for hanging in no matter what they hell they said! "Yeah, that part!" FHO Atl GA HNIC!

DEDICATION

This book is dedicated to:

My daughter Tanisha and my grandson. To you, my loves, I give my heart and soul.

The extended family of the Mighty Black Sabbath Motorcycle Club Nation

Paul 'Pep' Perry the Father, and Original 7 founding member

Leonard Mack founder of the Minneapolis, Minnesota chapter R.I.P.

Tia 'Red Bone' Purdue; Hey Driver from Brother, are we are friends yet?

A Sgt-at-Arms lives to serve the MC

A Sgt-at-Arms handles grievances expeditiously

A Sgt-at-Arms enforces traditions, protocols and regalia

A Sgt-at-Arms maintains absolute order in meetings

A Sgt-at-Arms is always disciplined with a level head

A Sgt-at-Arms learns expertise in conflict resolution

A Sgt-at-Arms sets the time for arrival and departure

A Sgt-at-Arms ensures no uniform violations among members

A Sgt-at-Arms always protects the President

A Sgt-at-Arms treats everyone fairly

A Sgt-at-Arms listens to both sides of the story

A Sgt-at-Arms doesn't take sides in MC politics

A Sgt-at-Arms does an investigation before forming an opinion

A Sgt-at-Arms is the reigning authority of bylaws knowledge

A Sgt-at-Arms is an expert MC historian

A Sgt-at-Arms knows the temperature of the Set

A Sgt-at-Arms resolves all internal MC conflicts

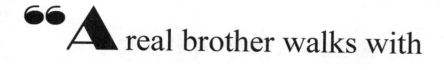

A real brother walks with

you when the rest of

the world walks away!

SARGENT-AT-ARMS BIBLE

"SOLDIER-SERGEANT OF THE BROTHERHOOD"

By:
JOHN EDWARD BUNCH II
Black Dragon
National President
Mighty Black Sabbath Motorcycle Club Nation
A Breed Apart
Since 1974 and Still Strong............................///
www.blacksabbathmc.com
www.blacksabbathmagazine.com
blackdragon@prospectbible.com

LOVE, HONOR, PERSEVERANCE, DUTY, COURAGE, LOYALTY...

Edited by:
- Christin Chapman
- Tanisha N. Bunch

First Edition, First Printing January 2017
www.sergeantatarmsbible.com

PREFACE

The Sergeant-at-Arms is the supreme servant of the MC. He utilizes his wisdom and experience to guide and protect the MC while it weathers the storms and challenges presented from within the brotherhood and without. There aren't many training tools available to prepare brothers for this office, nor can one find a truly complete job description written. Without a Master Sergeant to train his replacement, many MC Sergeants-at-Arms are doomed to muddle their way through their terms of office, trying their best to get a hand on the many complexities they face, while never quite conquering it all. Sergeant-at-Arms is a tough job that requires a solid brother to competently perform his duties. **SERGEANT-AT-ARMS BIBLE** presents a new perspective from which to approach aspects of the job one may not have previously considered.

The opinions in this book are mine, based on my experiences and values and how I think the Sergeant-at-Arms position should be run. They aren't the only opinions out there. There are others. You should gather as many opinions as you feel necessary—then take the best of each and apply it to your own situation. No one person knows everything about anything.

Overview

SERGEANT-AT-ARMS BIBLE was written to give guidance and reference to those executing their duties as the Sergeant-at-Arms of their beloved MC brotherhood. From the outset I will advise that different MCs will execute this position in slightly different ways which means that there may be more or less to the actual job than one will find within the pages of this book. The Sergeant-at-Arms exact duties will be outlined in their MC's bylaws so it's okay if there isn't 100% agreement with everything I say. I simply draw upon my 27 years of experience as a full patch in my 44-year-old National MC. So simply think of this book as a guide from whence you can glean knowledge and inspiration to help you perform your duties better than you did before you read it, rather than as a word-for-word gospel of how things **MUST** be done. Still I have listed what I have found to be BEST PRACTICES utilized by Sergeants-at-Arms professionals in all kinds of organizations universally, as well as those used in the MC. This to give you well rounded information and experiences to allow you to elevate your office to the highest possible levels. Raise the bar! You will be glad you did.

How to Use this Book

SERGEANT-AT-ARMS BIBLE can be read sequentially or randomly. If a particular area of interest or subject of reference is needed, simply go to that part of the book to glean. Each chapter stands on its own so it doesn't matter where one enters or exits the book. Also do not be afraid to utilize new ideas encountered within these pages even if they are unfamiliar. Growth often stems from an open mind willingly traversing unfamiliar territory. Furthermore, one should not pass up the opportunity to reevaluate, experiment, and fine tune processes discovered here. If something works better for a particular MC's situation one shouldn't hesitate to use it! Finally do not allow unfamiliarity or blind adherence to tradition impede implementation of excellent ideas. Advance the MC!

Make it Happen

Though it is easy to simply read this book for posterity, general knowledge, or to gain an understanding of the Sergeant-at-Arms position, one cannot make positive changes within the brotherhood without taking action! Evoke movement, and progress for the club based upon the knowledge that has been learned through the sacrifice of exerting the effort to read, learn and become edified. Remember, once one knows better one must do better.

Being Sergeant-at-Arms

Exercise the position as Sergeant-at-Arms with command-authority and confidence. Do not be afraid of this job. The MC's bylaws establish the duties and responsibilities and implicitly the right for this legendary office to exist! The bylaws equip the Sergeant-at-Arms to move forward in the best interests of the brotherhood, without having to ask permission or seek anyone's permission to act. The Sergeant-at-Arms possesses the authority to move autonomously into action according to his understanding of the bylaws. Know that this is one of the most important positions in the MC and that all members will look to the Sergeant-at-Arms for strength, courage, safety, security, wisdom, and justice. Learn and exercise advanced skills in crisis management and conflict resolution make the role invaluable to the MC. Be superb in the execution of all of the duties and responsibilities to which you have been elected to exercise. For no matter what reason one has for taking the Sergeant-at-Arms position, even if you knew little, or nothing about the job when you were sworn in, none of that matters now because you are the Sergeant-at-Arms now! The only choice now is competence and success! The best of your abilities should suffice. If that is not good enough, get better! Make a positive impact and improve the quality of life for the full patches of the brotherhood. Be Sergeant-at-Arms!

CONTENTS

CHAPTER 1:
HISTORY OF THE SERGEANT-AT-ARMS

To further appreciate the strength and responsibility this office wields and the mandate placed heavily upon the shoulders of Soldier-Sergeant, one would do well to look into the history of the world's Sergeant's-at-Arms. This universally respected office has roots that reach deeply into the history of brothers combined to achieve one cause in peace and armed conflict. It is from the needs of many to form the one, to come together as their brother's keepers, that this officer's authority was forged:

ser·geant-at-arms

/ˌsärjəntət ˈärmz/

noun: **serjeant-at-arms**

1. An official of a legislative or other assembly whose duty includes maintaining order and security.
2. British *historical.* A knight or armed officer in the service of the monarch or a lord.
3. A **Serjeant-at-Arms**, or **Sergeant-at-Arms** is an officer appointed by a deliberative body, usually a legislature, to keep order during its meetings. The word "**serjeant**" is derived from the Latin serviens, which means "servant".
4. The fourth officer in line to the succession of the presidency of a traditional motorcycle club, whose duties include maintaining order, accountability and security.

    Note: *May not be the fourth in succession in your MC.*

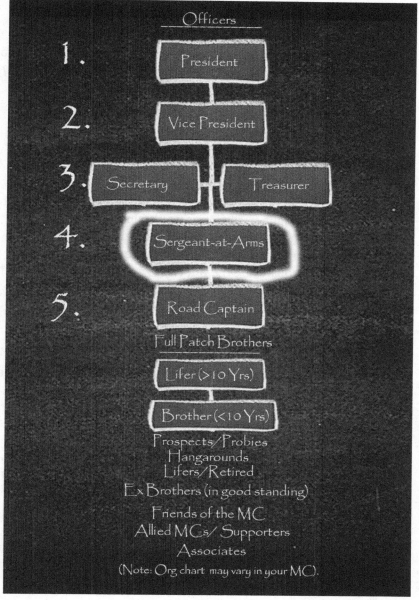

Origins of the Sergeant-at-Arms

The origins of the term "serjeant" hold four main definitions throughout its storied history; the first a *military rank,* the second a *law-enforcement* capacity, the third a *bodyguard* or *close personal escort* and the fourth *governmental/administrative* role.

Technically the four roles were not mutually exclusive, they were; however, very different in scope and responsibility.

Origins of the Military Sergeant-at-Arms

The Soldier-Sergeant was a man of middle class, fulfilling a junior role to a knight in medieval hierarchy. Soldier-Sergeants could fight either as heavy-to-light cavalry or as well-trained professional infantry, either as spearmen or crossbowmen. Medieval mercenaries often fell into the sergeant class and were seen as reliable quality troops. The sergeant class were deemed to be worth half of a knight in military value—though as light or heavy cavalry they were perhaps worth more than half because of the heavy expense to equip them.

Origins of the Law Enforcement Sergeant-at-Arms

The class was also used in England to serve the Sovereign in a police role, much like a bailiff in more recent times. Initially personal attendants were assigned to the Monarch. They were called "serjeanties" and were charged with providing services like the provision of arrows, fodder and waiting upon the Sovereign at table.[4] As the responsibilities expanded trusted "serjeanties" were permanently retained by the Monarch and advanced to the rank of "serjeants". "Serjeants" were required to be in immediate attendance on the Sovereign's person, specifically charged with arresting treason suspects and traitors, collecting loans, impressing men and ships into service, and serving as local administrators much like modern-day constables.

John E. Bunch II 'Black Dragon' BSFFBS

(http://www.aph.gov.au/About_Parliament/House_of_Representati
ves/Serjeant-at-Arms) [2].

Origins of the Body Guard Sergeant-at-Arms

The Serjeants-At-Arms constitute the oldest royal bodyguard in
England, dating from the time of King Richard I (around 1189) as a
formed body and close personal escort. [1] The title "Sergeant-at-
Arms" appears during the crusades in the reign of King Philip II of
France in 1192 [1]. Richard I had twenty-four serjeants with him on
the Crusades. In 1278 they were formed into a twenty-strong Corps
of Serjeants-at-Arms by King Edward I and served as a mounted
close escort. In 1399, King Richard II limited the corps to thirty
serjeants, and King Charles II had sixteen. The number was reduced
to eight in 1685 and since then has gradually declined. [1]

Origins of the Governmental Sergeant-at-Arms

The formal role of a modern governmental/administrative
Sergeants-at-Arms in legislative bodies is to keep order during
meetings, and, if necessary, forcibly remove any members who are
overly rowdy or disruptive. They perform a number of
administrative and custodial duties but their jobs can still put them
in harm's way, just as if they were still Soldier-Sergeants on
medieval battlefields because one of their primary responsibilities is
ensuring the safety and security of the legislative bodies they serve.
In fact in 2014 Canadian Parliament Sergeant-at-Arms Kevin Vickers
fearlessly engaged in a gunfight with a cowardly terrorist that
attacked the Canadian House of Commons in a hail-storm of gunfire,
after murdering Canadian soldier Corporal Natan Cirillo [4] who was
standing guard at Canada's war memorial[4]. Vickers acted heroically
along with Royal Canadian Mounted Police (RCMP) Constable Curtis
Barrett who eliminated the cowardly terrorist. Vickers, who had
previously been an RMCP constable for twenty-nine years, attaining

the rank of Chief Superintendent, transformed into that "Soldier-Sergeant" of yesteryear instantly, risking his life to protect the legislative family under his charge. He was awarded with the Star of Courage along with six others involved in bringing the incident under control. Eight others were awarded the Medal of Bravery. It is clear to see that the Sergeant-at-Arms has many duties above and beyond that for which he is typically known; organizing meetings, following protocols and keeping members in order.

United Kingdom Government Sergeant-at-Arms
In 1415, the British House of Commons received its first Sergeant-at-Arms. Since then the serjeant has been a royal appointment as one of the Sovereign's Serjeants-at-Arms responsible for certain administrative and custodial functions, as well as security within the chamber of the House. The House of Lords has a similar officer.

United States Government Sergeant-At-Arms
The First Congress (1789–1791) adopted many of the traditions of colonial parliamentary bodies and the British Parliament, including the inclusion of the Sergeant-at-Arms office. The formal role of a Sergeant-at-Arms in modern U.S. legislative bodies is to keep order during meetings, if necessary, forcibly remove any members who are overly rowdy or disruptive, compel senators or representatives to attend sessions they are boycotting, arrest individuals who violate senate or house rules, and provide security for the legislative assemblies. There is an office for a Sergeant-at-Arms for both legislative bodies.

Sergeant-at-Arms 'Doorkeeper' of the Senate
The Sergeant-at-Arms of the Senate is the highest ranking Federal Law Enforcement Officer in the Senate of the United States. When the first Congress convened in 1789, this office was originally called "Doorkeeper of the Senate." The Office of Doorkeeper was

established to address the single most pressing problem confronting the Senate at its birth - its inability to keep a majority of members in the Capitol long enough to organize and begin the business of government. A doorkeeper was also necessary to control access to the Senate sessions, which were private for the first six years. Later, when the sessions were open to the public, the doorkeeper was responsible for maintaining order on the floor of the Senate and in the galleries (http://www.senate.gov/reference/office/sergeant_at_arms.htm). This title remained unchanged from the First Congress until the Eighth Congress (April 7, 1789 – March 3, 1803). The title "Doorkeeper" was replaced with Sergeant-at-Arms to reflect the expanded administrative duties of the position [4]. The Sergeant-at-Arms is also the executive officer for the Senate and provides Senators with computers, equipment, repairs and security services [5].

The Sergeant-at-Arms of the House of Representatives

The Sergeant-at-Arms of the House of Representatives also dates back to the First Congress as the chamber's principle law enforcement official, charged with maintaining security on the floor and for the House-side of the Capitol complex. A total of 36 individuals have served as the House Sergeant-at-Arms since 1789. Mandated under the current House Rule II, the Sergeant-at-Arms of the House also enforces protocol and ensures decorum during floor proceedings. Over time, the office's duties have encompassed administrative functions: arranging Capitol funerals, managing parking facilities, and issuing identification to House members and staff.

Government Sergeant-at-Arms in other Countries

Many other countries around the world have Sergeants-at-Arms employed in their legislative bodies including: Australia, Bangladesh, Canada, New Zealand, South Africa, Sri Lanka and others.

Admin Sergeants-at-Arms Worldwide

The position of Sergeant-at-Arms is popular today in all types of organizations, including: fraternities, sororities, social clubs, masonic lodges, charities, law enforcement bodies, MCs and many others. The position still bears the hallmark of confidence, wisdom and safety that it has since the medieval times of the Soldier-Sergeant employed in service of his Lord. Today's Sergeant-at-Arms is used mostly to enforce bylaws, protocols and traditions of his organizations. They are also used to enforce their institutions' accountability systems and run elections. These kinds of administrative duties are standard among modern Sergeants-at-Arms. But of course in MC brotherhoods; and other brotherhoods there are slight differences...

CHAPTER 2:
MOTORCYCLE CLUB SERGEANT-AT-ARMS

The Motorcycle Club Sergeant-at-Arms is a powerful, authoritarian figure. As the worldwide history of his position reflects, he draws his influence and authority from centuries of similar "Serjeants" who have served their institutions with honor, dignity, strength and respect before him. The Sergeant-at-Arms is the primary organizer and overseer of the accountability system within the MC. He maintains proper order within MC meetings and ensures that the bylaws and rules concerning the MC's uniforms, colors and images are observed. He adjudicates disciplinary judicial boards and all associated processes. He also provides the physical security of the MC.

MC Sergeant-at-Arms Authority

Under his authority he shall ensure:

- Bylaws and standing rules are strictly enforced
- Traditions, ceremonies, regalia and pageantries are not abandoned
- Discipline, sanctions, suspensions and fines are meted out
- Orders of the Executive Committee are carried out in an expeditious manner
- Events run smoothly by policing them and keeping order
- Safety and security of the MC on and off the Set
- Defense of the MC against its enemies
- Physical security of the MC's President and senior officers
- Due process is guaranteed to all members

Accomplishing His Duties

To accomplish his duties the Sergeant-at-Arms shall:

- Conscript (deputize) members to aid in keeping order within or without the MC when necessary
- Report any violations of the MC's bylaws as well as unseemly behavior or incidents to the Executive Committee
- Confiscate the MC's insignia and colors from any member(s) who retires, resigns, is suspended, or is expelled from the MC
- Keep and maintain a record of all data pertinent to the safety and security of the MC
- Upon becoming aware of any real or perceived threats to the MC, immediately notify the Executive Committee of that information and employ plans for the defense of the MC

War Chief

The MC Sergeant-at-Arms is also a war chief of his organization. Like that Soldier-Sergeant of medieval times, he represents the power, autonomy, accountability and the resolve of the MC!

All-Encompassing Role with Four Heads

When it comes down to it the MC Sergeant-at-Arms has an all-encompassing role that bears responsibility on four equally important fronts:

- *Administrative (day-to-day running of the MC)*
- *Constable (enforcing bylaws and regalia)*
- *Security (physical protection of the President and Brothers)*

- **Martial (protects the MC's autonomy against threats)**

He must be technically proficient in executing all of them because weakness or incompetence in any area could mean the doom of the brotherhood.

Building the Knowledge

As one begins to expand their knowledge of what is required of this position the very first lesson as Sergeant-at-Arms, is to learn how to love the full patch brothers more than love of one's self. One's entire Sergeant-at-Arms' career, if it is to be successful, will hinge upon his ability to put the best interests of the MC above his own. He will have to love more than a back patch. He will have to love the people represented by that patch. A patch does not make an MC. The members make the MC. The MC is about the people who make up its membership. Love the brothers and love of the MC brotherhood will be automatic. Love the MC and always represent that patch with honor. The Sergeant-at-Arms is responsible for their safety, security and the quality of their MC lives. Do the job!

Minimum Qualifications

The job requires a full patch brother with a level head and a high degree of integrity, discipline, maturity, loyalty and dedication. It is not normally a job for "newbies" or "hotheads" and requires a skilled journeymen with club and MC Set experience, possessing many forged relationships and the respect of the MC community at large. The minimum qualifications you should bring to this position are:

- An unmatched knowledge and understanding of your MC's bylaws, history, purpose, mission statement, and goals of its founding fathers
- An expert level understanding and knowledge of the MC set and MC protocol
- Ability to maintain a pleasant but stern demeanor in all situations
- Ability to maintain control of his emotions throughout difficult situations
- Ability to keep peace at the meetings
- Ability to focus on the big picture
- Excellent conflict resolution skills
- Ability to make difficult decisions, under pressure, fairly and without bias

The Sergeant-at-Arms will be an unsung hero and arguably the most hardcore, hard-nosed, dog-eared officer of the MC. He can also expect to be one of the most hated officers in the MC, just like the police are hated in the streets. He will be hated because he is the internal police of the MC. But he should fear not you because he is also the most beloved and needed brother when he comes running to the rescue of the same brother who hated him yesterday.

Sergeant-at-Arms Matrix of Responsibility

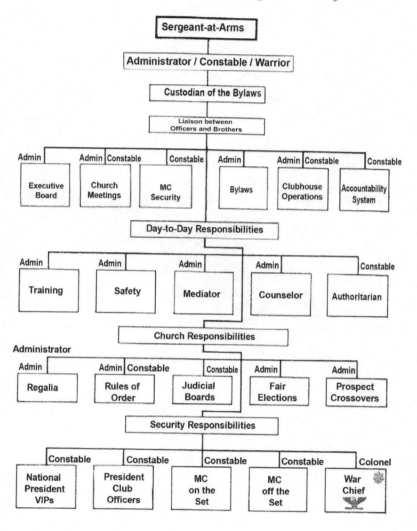

PART I SGT-AT-ARMS THE ADMINISTRATOR

BYLAWS

Bylaws are the glue that hold these diverse men together in one brotherhood. They guarantee the fair and ethical treatment of all who pledge themselves to this extended family. They are comprised of the voting will of all brothers in good standing. They represent the values, convictions, and traditions of our mighty MC brotherhood. The bylaws prevent arbitrary rules from being 'invented' for the expediency of one President or another who may come into or leave office. They may only be amended via our accepted processes which no one man may alter. Bylaws are the foundation of conduct upon which our brotherhood was built, to which we have established our lifelong commitment. They are to be revered as our sacred covenant to one another and the covenant established between the MC and WE the full patch brothers. They define our responsibilities and guarantee our rights. Therefore no brother may be held above our sacred bylaws. To the bylaws every brother must acquiesce.

...And the **KEEPER** of our sacred covenant shall now and forever be the;

Sergeant-at-Arms

CHAPTER 3:
LEADERSHIP

Supervisor/Manager/Executive Board

The Sergeant-at-Arms is a member of the executive board. He is one of the top five officers of the MC. He advises the President as to the condition of the men, as well as, votes on issues pertinent to the executive board. Initially it can be difficult for a new Sergeant-at-Arms, to advance from the ranks of club brother to senior officer. It means he must disassociate himself from the 'clicks' to which he may have previously been aligned, so that he can now work to further the best interests of the MC and support the President, and executive board. The Sergeant-at-Arms must remain neutral in all politics and club conflicts so that he can operate his office fairly.

"Best for the MC" as used in the concept of this book has two meanings:

1. Best interests of the executive board, those who are actually responsible for carrying out the decisions derived from the voting body of the brotherhood, and the orders issued by the President.
2. Best interest of the President's way of getting things done (management). In most situations he will fall on the side of management because the duly elected leader of the MC is most often the best at accomplishing the club's goals—and the Sergeant-at-Arms is part of the management team. He must also be an effective manager. Management is the art and science of directing the will, materials, human power, ideas and concepts of the brotherhood into actual movement towards

accomplishing goals for the benefit of the brotherhood. When a brother advances from brother to Sergeant-at-Arms he no longer focuses on personally doing the work necessary to move the agenda of the brotherhood forward, instead he focuses on getting others to combine their efforts to do this work. The Sergeant-at-Arms is the leader-manager of the MC's efforts towards strength, security, peace, and quality of life. As such he must learn to become a master at human relations.

Provide Support to the President

For any organization to be strong its leader must be obeyed. The MC is no exception. Even though the MC brotherhood is a democratic body that runs by the vote, executed by an executive board, it does have an executive officer. That officer is the MC's President. In a traditional MC he is empowered by the bylaws to make certain decisions on his own. His orders must therefore be carried out expeditiously and completely. The Sergeant-at-Arms ensures the leadership of the president remains strong and absolute. He will stand in stark opposition to members who try to undermine the authority of the sitting President. He will severely punish any threat to the office of the Presidency or any fool who would show insubordination or disrespect to a sitting President during any church service or other MC gathering.

Supporting the President through a Coup D'état

The Sergeant-at-Arms should always support the President during any coup attempt. Coups begin as nasty little conspiracies that evolve into illegal actions (illegal = against the MC's bylaws) used to snatch power from the President, usually before his term of office is complete. The Sergeant-at-Arms simply cannot allow a coup to stand because it is an incredible threat to the stability of the MC. The bylaws give a President absolute authority to operate his MC. Any illegal attempt to overthrow his leadership must be fought vigorously by the Sergeant-at-Arms because if actors can depose the office of the President then any member of the MC is vulnerable and its bylaws are worthless. For the security of all brothers of the MC the Sergeant-at-Arms is duty bound to root out and destroy conspirators' ability to cause the MC that kind of harm. Even if the Sergeant-at-Arms does not like the President he can never be in league with conspirators. He must punish them ruthlessly and remove them from the MC with extreme prejudice. The Sergeant-at-Arms will ensure the peaceful transition of power within the MC, according to the bylaws and terms of office. He will ensure that proper charges are brought and procedures followed in all cases. He is the enforcer of the law and can hold no one above it.

coup d'é·tat

ˌko͞o dāˈtä/

another term for coup.
unpunctuated: **coup détat**; noun: **coup d'état**; plural noun: **coup d'états**
coup /ko͞o/: a sudden, violent, and illegal seizure of power from a government.

Supporting the Bylaws over the President

Though the Sergeant-at-Arms supports the authority of the office of the President let there be no misunderstanding that he supports that authority only in as much as that authority is exercised within the concepts of, and the spirit of the MC's bylaws. The Sergeant-at-Arms is not the watchdog of the President used to attack his political rivals. The Sergeant's-at-Arms office is not to be used for retribution against brothers or to empower a would-be dictator gone mad with the lust for power. The Sergeant-at-Arms is not the "wingman" of the President. On the contrary the Sergeant-at-Arms ensures that no brother stands above the bylaws. He stands as the chief law enforcement officer of the MC. He will advise the President on matters where the President may want to implement his ideas. He will express his opinion as to whether those ideas are legal according to the bylaws, illegal, or fall within a gray area. He will always seek to guide the President away from gray areas, inappropriate areas and areas that are implicitly illegal according to the bylaws.

Liaison

No Sergeant-at-Arms can be respected if doesn't know the basic components of the tasks that must be performed under his leadership. The Sergeant-at-Arms must know thoroughly all of the jobs that must be performed to make the MC function. He will know how each component functions and how to get the best out of his members.

As the chain of command goes, most direction from the executive board will come down to the brothers through the Sergeant-at-Arms. In this way he is the only officer that will have daily contact with the brothers. Requests to and from the brotherhood to gain an audience with the senior levels of the MC must channel through him. He therefore has the pulse of the MC and knows the operating temperature. Equally the Sergeant-at-Arms is in direct contact with Management on a daily basis. He is the conduit through which the senior officers speak to the rank and file brothers. Therefore he knows the operating temperature of the executive board as well. He is the liaison between the brother officers and the brothers. If he is competent he will successfully keep them cohesive and responding well to achieve the objectives of the MC. He does this best not by being a rhetorical repeating device that can only read bylaws and shout out orders, instead he learns people. He learns how they react under pressure and he learns how to work with them to achieve their best.

Concepts of Organization

The Sergeant-at-Arms should toil to obtain a working knowledge of the concepts of the internal organization of the MC, to better understand how he can utilize the chain of command to appropriately manage and solve brothers' personal situations, club crisis, and to see club events to successful conclusions. Understanding the logic behind the MC's chain of command and officer responsibilities allows him to better appreciate the differences between officer, senior brother, junior brother, prospect, hang-around and supporter functions within the MC hierarchy. The Sergeant-at-Arms should intimately know the functions of every role within the MC as he is the liaison between the top and the bottom.

President

The "Prez" is the leader of the chapter. He is the MC's figurehead and is usually the spokesman when dealing with law enforcement or the media. He is the chairman at club meetings and represents the chapter at national meetings.

Vice President

The "VP" is second in command and fills in when the President is away. As the executive officer it is his responsibility to make sure that matters passed at church are carried out satisfactorily. He is second in line to succession if the President can no longer perform his duties.

Secretary

The Secretary is responsible for the MC's documents. He keeps minutes of meetings and records dates of significant events, such as anniversaries, prospect crossovers, charitable activities, etc. He corresponds with other MC's and apprises the MC of communications received from other MC's. He keeps brothers informed of upcoming events and keeps record of the MC's assets if the treasurer is not charged with that duty.

Note: Some MC's have a Business Manager and/or Public Relations Officer (PRO) that may split some of these responsibilities.

Treasurer

The Treasurer handles the MC's money. He's in charge of collecting club dues (donations) and funds of any kind. He also pays the MC's bills. All debts owed to the MC are paid to the treasurer. He will also oversee and advise the MC about any available business opportunities prior to any decisions.

Note: In some traditional MC's the position of Treasurer and Secretary are combined. Other MC's have a Business Manager position that may split some of these responsibilities.

Sergeant-at-Arms

The Sergeant-at-Arms is the enforcer of the MC's bylaws, protocols, traditions and sovereignty. He maintains order at club meetings and ensures formality. He is responsible for the physical security of the clubhouse, the MC and the President—especially while on the Set. He also conducts the MC's wars, if there are any.

Road Captain

The Road Captain is in charge of moving the MC pack from one destination to another in an orderly and safe manner. He manages the logistics of the MC during runs. He plans the route and organizes refueling stops and rest breaks. The Road Captain rides at the front and leads the pack with the President. In many MC's the Road Captain is a "non-executive board" officer; however the Road Captain is regarded as the "President" when the pack is on the road and moving.

Life Members (Active/Inactive)

A "Lifer" is a senior full patch brother who has met the club's requirements to be designated "brother-for-life" which could mean that he met a time requirement (like ten years), because of his contributions to the club, or some other qualifying factors. Lifers have the right to take part in the running of the club; however, their attendance at meetings and club events may not be compulsory. Lifers may or may not be active but may still be able to vote regardless (depending upon the MC). They will always retain their colors because they are technically a part of the MC until death.

Full Patch Brothers

Full Patch Brothers are members of the MC who have earned the right to wear the colors after successfully prospecting. They take part in the running of the club and attend church regularly. They are commonly referred to as "members" or, in some clubs, "patches."

Prospects

A Prospect or "Probie" is a probationary member of the MC who has yet to earn his full patch. Although some MC's would not call them "members" they still wear some aspect of the MC's colors, are responsible for the bylaws, and even pay dues in some MCs— although they do not get the right to vote and most cannot attend church or a full church service unless invited for a purpose. Prospects are expected to do what they are told and follow the orders of full patch brothers. They are to be silent at all times unless spoken to, and many MCs do not permit them to utilize any name other than "Prospect" (i.e. "My name is Prospect 13."). There is no time period on how long a person may be a Prospect unless stated in the MC's bylaws.

Hang-Arounds

A Hang-around hopes to become a prospective member of the MC and enters a formal stage known as the "hang-around period." In this stage he works to become known by all members before being voted in as a Prospect. A good Hang-around immediately immerses himself into the MC's life by volunteering and helping to do menial tasks. This demonstrates his discipline and determination to get into his prospecting period. There is no time period on how long a person may be a Hang-around unless stated in the MC's bylaws.

Ex-Members

When a full patch brother leaves the MC it's either "In Good Standing" or on bad terms. Former brothers who leave in good standing may do so for many reasons where a leave of absence is not viable, such as employment, injury, illness, family obligations, incarceration, or personal crisis. In such cases former brothers in good standing usually remain close associates of the MC and often provide valuable assistance when needed.

Friends of the MC/Allied Clubs/Supporters

"Friends of the MC" are allied MCs, close supporters and female support social clubs. They normally have an official obligation of support to the MC and the bonds are often as close as family. They are often referred to as "brother" or "sister" clubs.

Associates

"Associates" of the MC are persons or clubs who are less formally linked to the MC, but support its activities, functions, parties, charitable pursuits and get-togethers.

Note: *There are other officer positions inside MCs such as Business Manager, PRO, Nomad, and Enforcer as well as national positions like, National President. This book is not exhaustive in its effort to list all positions and titles.*

Sergeant-at-Arms as a Club Leader

The Sergeant-at-Arms will find the men ready to accept him as a leader the moment he takes office. The popularity and respect for the history of his office among the brothers will make him an instant star but whether or not he maintains that respect relies on his ability to successfully perform as a leader.

Shakespeare said of men that "some are born great, some achieve greatness, and some have greatness thrust upon them." The same can be said about leaders. Some men are born leaders and fall into leadership easily without much effort. They are a whiz at it and others accept their leadership without question. Some men, acquire the leadership through study, observation, formal training, and trial and error. Only through hard work and diligent, progressive behavior do they achieve a leader position, relying on their track record of increased responsibilities. Finally, some men are thrust into leadership through some unforeseen event which requires them to reach inside themselves to find leadership qualities they never knew existed. They solve the crisis and continue on in their new leadership role effectively. It really doesn't matter from which category one comes, the fact is that no matter how hard one has to work to be a leader, or if one really doesn't have to work that hard at all, once one finds themselves in the position—it is time to excel. When brothers are under the guidance of a good leader they show it. The brotherhood becomes a cohesive unit that rides together, hangs out together and enjoys the fellowship of each other's company. They protect one another and stand as one through times of crisis. Brothers go out of their way to do things for certain officers while other officers have little impact on the conduct of the MC at all. They carry out instructions cheerfully and contribute more than what is expected when they feel like they are part of the team, that they are working to make the MC great, and that their contributions are appreciated. It takes competent, skillful leadership to achieve these kinds of results from the brothers. The Sergeant-at-Arms will be a team builder who can drive the men to feel exuberant about their extended family. The morale of the men will be high and they will be proud to please their successful Sergeant-at-Arms.

What is Leadership

Leadership is the ability to get other people to perform tasks willingly through influence or example. Leadership is about mastering relationships and influencing people towards performing good deeds and putting forth one's best efforts. There are certain characteristics of a good leader:

- Genuinely likes people
- Interact well with people fluidly
- Enjoys developing/training people under his guidance
- Is direct and stern when need be
- Is about the brotherhood's business in all aspects
- Possesses a sense of fairness
- Possesses a sense moral courage
- Possesses humanity towards others
- Is self-deprecating while being strongly confident
- Possesses a sense of humor
- Possesses a strong devotion to duty
- Sees things for what they are not for what he'd like them to be
- Possesses an understanding of human nature
- Is hard to impress
- Is not disillusioned by the bad acts of others
- Does not prejudge/allows everyone to start with a clean slate
- Expertly enlists others in cooperation and effort in a common cause
- Seeks expertise in matter in which he is not strong

What is expected from the Sergeant-at-Arms

Club brothers expect to have good working relationships with the officers above them. They want to believe the MC cares about them and that their home within the extended family is secure. The Sergeant-at-Arms represents the strength and security of the MC; therefore if he is solid, the brothers, subordinate to him, and the executive board, senior to him, will be solid. The MC expects:

- The Sergeant-at-Arms to know his job
- Courteous and consistent treatment
- Provides the necessary instructions to accomplish tasks
- Fair play—no favoritism
- Opportunity to talk things over without fear of reprisal
- Understanding the brother's problems
- Prompt handling of the brother's grievances
- Letting brothers know where they stand with him
- Adequate representation of the brother's points of view
- Recognition of the brothers for a job well done
- Taking each brother's problem as an individual situation
- Rewarding brothers for contributions of excellence

Get to Know the Job

There is a level of respect afforded people who know their jobs and seem to know exactly what to do no matter what situation arises. They make things look easy because even when they don't have the answers the know how to get them. They prevent problems before they start and develop strategies to bring the MC to the next level. We call them journeymen.

Courteous and Consistent Treatment

My grandma used to say, "Son, you catch more flies with honey than you do with vinegar." Not to say that vinegar doesn't catch flies, but if one wants to catch a whole lot of them it would seem that honey is the ingredient that should dispatched. Such can be said about consistent and courteous treatment. When we look at cars in an intersection, we can see courtesy at play. Drivers seem to instinctively know that allowing every other car to pass is not only the courteous thing to do but it allows traffic to flow smoothly and efficiently. We can see drivers falling into the pattern without a traffic cop on the scene. It isn't until the one jerk shows up and decides to go out of turn that the horns start honking and everything gets messed up. Courtesy saves time and wear and tear on one's nerves. It also eliminates initial opposition to authority on the part of independent thinking, alpha-male club brothers. Look at courtesy like motor oil—the lubricant of goodwill, to see brothers as individuals, putting oneself in a club brother's place. It should be practiced consistently regardless if the Sergeant-at-Arms is in a good or bad mood. If practiced consistently the brothers will know how to take the Sergeant-at-Arms and can feel confident in their approach to interacting with him resolve problems or a job done.

Fair Play

There is nothing that tears the moral of the MC down quicker than a brother, or a group of brothers, feeling that someone else got a better outcome, better deal, or got away with something where others would be held accountable or not get such a great deal in a similar situation. Showing favoritism is a sure way to create ill will in the brotherhood. All brothers' eyes are on the Sergeant-at-Arms at all times, so if there is the look of impropriety it will be known all over the MC instantly. He should make it his common practice never to show favoritism and treat all equally, even though it may be difficult or politically inexpedient. If the brothers feel that the Sergeant-at-Arms will always be fair they will trust him, respect him and honor his decisions—even when his decisions might not return their expected results. They know he treats everyone the same.

Politics Verses Fair Play

When I was in the United States Submarine Navy in the 1990s, for a time, I was stationed at Submarine Training Facility San Diego (SUBTRAFACSD), California as a Master Training Specialist (the highest level of achievement awarded a Technical Trainer/Instructor in the U.S. Navy at that time). I was assigned as an Instructor in a department that was charged with handling top secret classified materials used to train prospective submarine Commanding Officers. Our headquarters was a guarded building where every person in it had a top secret security clearance, even to gain entry. There, in a room where you had to have a top secret security clearance to enter, in a safe, that you had to have a top secret combination and two people to open, were documents we used as reference materials to train our students to fight submarine warfare. I can remember a couple of my shipmates made minor mistakes and left one of those safes open. The result was that they lost their entire careers. In a safe behind cipher locks, in secured rooms with no windows, in a building where every person had security clearances and guards controlled every entry, a guy makes a small mistake and loses everything he worked for over the previous 15 years. But that was how it was and those were the rules by which we lived. We understood that any mistakes made while handling classified materials were immediately career ending—and could possibly wind up with a jail sentence. You see we took an oath to defend the secrets of the United States with our lives if need be. Fast-forward nearly 20 years to the election of 2016. When a candidate that was running for President was shown to have mishandled classified materials, as Secretary of State, and did not receive a similar punishment like the shipmates I served with all those years ago. I was quite angry because there was a difference in the punishment handed out by the government, if any. After the race was won and the new President Elect announced that he was considering a retired general, for Secretary of State, who had plead guilty and was sentenced for the improper handling of classified materials— my blood was again brought to a boiling point. Such consideration was never given to my shipmates who had served their country with honor and distinction up until their mistakes! Why were these people, who held the highest ranks of responsibility in guarding our nation's secrets, not being held to the same standards that my lowly E-6 shipmates were held to when their careers were destroyed for making honest mistakes infinitesimally smaller than the intentional mistakes made by these two? The answer is really two-fold: politics and a level of responsibility. Could those E-6s run an entire country as Secretary of State? Never. There is an undeniable fact that, because of their positions in life, people with heavier responsibilities are allowed to make larger mistakes with fewer apparent consequences. Consider this, will the President of the MC receive the same consequence for being late to a meeting a Prospect receives? Perhaps the President just got out of a regional meeting with a dominant he was unable to avoid because of the importance of that meeting to the MC. As

Sergeant-at-Arms being fair is not always easy. One will be required to make difficult decisions during their service as Sergeant-at-Arms. For example what if the President of the MC borrowed money out of an account he should not have touched, but put the money back soon after, yet the action was still discovered. This situation could present problems that aren't always so black and white. Let's add to the equation that the clubhouse is in the President's name and if he is taken down, perhaps the whole MC falls. Now the MC looks at the Sergeant-at-Arms to restore order. He is facing one side of the MC that finds no foul in what the President did and wants him to stay, while also dealing with the other side that wants the bylaws enforced and wants him to leave no matter what the cost to the brotherhood. What should he do? Politics will come into play in many decisions and how one must react is not something any book can teach. The responsibility of the Sergeant-at-Arms is to maintain the strength of the MC. It must survive no matter what. It's easy to say "Be fair and treat everyone the same" like it's the most simple thing in the world to do. But when situations presented are gray instead of black and white, the Sergeant-at-Arms must make a decision that can threaten his own position. If ever caught between a rock and a hard place—the Sergeant-at-Arms should always choose what is in the best interest of the MC.

Opportunity to Talk Things Over

An excellent Sergeant-at-Arms will always be highly sought after for his opinion on any manner of things that have nothing to do with his position as an officer. Brothers will want to discuss personal situations, employment issues, marital problems, extramarital affairs, problems with addictions, and a host of other matters both good and bad. And they will also want to be heard when it comes to matters of the MC. Sometimes they will want to hear one's opinion and other times they just want to be heard. Several traits of trusted Sergeants-at-Arms:

1. Possesses the confidence of others.
2. Others value his advice and judgement.
3. He is a good listener and has a capacity for understanding.
4. He does not pass judgement.
5. He can just listen without always giving an opinion.

Prompt Handling of Grievances

A grievance is anything that adversely affects a brother's attitude towards the MC brotherhood. His cause may be real or imaginary; it may arise from conditions within the MC or from home, work or the Set. But no matter what it is, to the brother who holds the grievance it is real and should never be minimized. Remember that a brother's grievance can run through the MC like a cancerous growth spreading from one brother to the next until it has the brotherhood churning round a self-destructive path to oblivion.

The two basic steps to handling a grievance are:

- Discovering the facts
- Doing something about the complaint

Remember that the brotherhood is a place where brothers find it difficult to "tattle" or "snitch", so if a brother is bringing an issue he must deem it to be important. Put the brother at ease when listening and hear his entire complaint. Do not rush him. Be attentive until the story is complete. Keep an open mind and investigate the facts entirely before coming to a conclusion. Do not immediately take the MC's side before conducting a fact finding mission, even if you believe that you have some familiarity with the subject. A decision can only be made with all of the facts.

CHAPTER 4:
CLUB MEETINGS (CHURCH SERVICE)

An MC's weekly or monthly meetings to handle routine club business, is commonly referred to as "attending, going to, or having Church." Church occurs at regular intervals established by the MC's bylaws. Because the truth and the light of what is happening in the MC, and events happening within the lives of its members, are addressed during Church, it is definitely easy to see why it is a sacred gathering in the MC world. As such it can also be quite a stormy gathering.

Cell Phones in Church

MCs are private societies and their business is not for outside consumption or discussion. Therefore, in most MCs, cell phones, recording devices, hidden cameras, etc., have no place in church. The Sergeant-at-Arms will collect such instruments before each gathering and monitor the proceedings for any unscrupulous brothers who might try to record a club meeting.

Weapons in Church

In some MCs all weapons are confiscated by the Sergeant-at-Arms before church begins. The reasons for this are obvious. Even though this practice may not be standard operating procedure for all MCs, the Sergeant-at-Arms may want to take this step when the meeting will discuss a particularly divisive issue, such as judicial board, discipline, suspension or expulsion hearing, etc.

Note: Some MCs remove colors before such meetings so there aren't fist fights to take them if the proceedings don't go well and someone gets kicked out.

Details of Church Service

Church happens differently for all MCs. Typical things you may see discussed are:

- planned events
- budgets
- elections
- chartable pursuits
- dances, annuals, and other celebrations
- rides, field meets, and conventions
- who is sick, healing, or deceased/funeral arrangements
- introduction of hang-arounds and prospects
- voting prospects into the MC
- voting on initiatives and motions
- disagreements or concerns with opposing MCs
- Pow Wows
- problems with law enforcement, government, or community organizations
- crisis management and problem solving
- disciplinary hearings and censures

The Sergeant-at-Arms ensures that Church is conducted orderly and according to tradition, while ensuring security and efficiency. The success of church is one of his most important and primary tasks.

Before Church Service

The Sergeant-at-Arms typically sets up the clubhouse or meeting place and checks that everything is in order before other full patch brothers arrive. If prospects are attending their first meeting, the Sergeant-at-Arms briefs their sponsors on protocol and procedures they must observe during church. He will administer sign-in documents, greet arriving members and VIPs, and ensure that the meeting starts on time.

During Church Service

The Sergeant-at-Arms keeps order. If full patch brothers or attendees are disruptive, the Sergeant may warn them, fine them, and/or eject them from the meeting—including suspend them or bring them up on charges as directed by the executive board and President. He may also perform other administrative tasks such as collecting ballots, tallying votes and recording attendance.

After Church Service

The Sergeant-at-Arms typically oversees the cleanup process after meetings, either alone or by directing prospects, hang-arounds, or junior brothers. He packs up equipment and materials and restores the clubhouse to its original state. He is responsible for the safe storage of any equipment, supplies and property owned by the MC – inventorying them after each meeting and reordering supplies when needed.

Additional Duties

The Sergeant-at-Arms is responsible for the MC's flag, colors and other ceremonial etiquette. For example, he may ensure that flags are correctly positioned and displayed and lead the MC brotherhood in the club's Pledge of Allegiance to start meetings.

Decorum at Church Service

Since the purpose of the church service is to reach agreements on MC actions, good taste demands that full patch brothers use the time for exactly this purpose. The Sergeant-at-Arms must prevent full patch brothers from abusing their undeniable right to speak, keeping repetition to a minimum. He should ensure that full patch brothers respect the rights and opinions of others and guide them in learning to be as good at losing as they are at winning. He must also convey a since of duty before each service, reinforcing to the brothers that they are in service for the purpose of bettering the MC and not for the purpose of furthering their personal agendas that don't coincide with the previous. Require the brothers to act in good taste throughout the entire meeting and punish them mightily if they fail in meeting that obligation.

What is Parliamentary Procedure

Parliamentary procedure is the body of rules, ethics, and customs governing meetings and other operations of clubs, organizations, legislative bodies, and deliberative assemblies. In the United States, parliamentary procedure is also referred to as "parliamentary". In the United Kingdom, Ireland, Australia, New Zealand, South Africa, and other English-speaking countries it is often called "chairmanship." At its heart, parliamentary procedure ensures the rule of the majority with respect for the minority. When used in a traditional MC the objective of parliamentary procedure is to allow deliberation upon questions of interest to the MC and to arrive at conclusion that serves the will of the MC. It is based on the principles of allowing the majority to make decisions effectively and efficiently (majority rule), while ensuring fairness towards the minority and giving each full patch brother the right to voice an opinion. Traditional MCs follow parliamentary procedure to debate and reach group decisions—with the least possible friction. Voting by the full patch brothers, in good standing, determines the will of the MC.

The parliamentary procedures rules of order can consist of rules written by the MC (sometimes included in the bylaws), but more often are supplemented by a published rules adopted by the MC. Typically, national, state and other full-scale legislative assemblies have extensive internally written rules of order, whereas non-legislative bodies or private societies, like the MC, will write or adopt a limited set of specific rules to meet their needs.

A parliamentary structure conducts the MC's business through motions, which cause actions. Full patch brothers, in good standing, bring business before the MC by introducing main motions or dispose of this business through subsidiary motions and incidental motions. Parliamentary procedure also allows for rules in regards to nomination, voting, disciplinary action, appeals, dues and drafting organization charters, constitutions and bylaws.

The Sergeant-at-Arms ensures the success of the goals of church through the system of parliamentary procedure.

History of Parliamentary Procedure

The term "parliamentary procedure" gets its name from its use in the parliamentary system of government. In the 16th and 17th century, there were rules of order in the early parliaments of England. In the 1560s Sir Thomas Smyth began the process of writing down accepted procedures and published a book about them for the House of Commons in 1583. Early rules included:

- Only one subject to be discussed at a time (adopted 1581)

- Personal attacks are to be avoided in debate (1604)
- Debate must be limited to the merits of the question (1610)
- Division of a question when some seem to be for one part but not the other (1640)

These were to be the basic rules and can still be employed with great success, in any MC meeting. I find it rather humorous that the problems we had in meetings in 1581 are the same problems we have in meetings today. But a successful Sergeant-at-Arms will strive to ensure these basic tenants of conducting productive meetings are employed:

1. Discussing only one subject at a time ensures efficient use of everyone's time, allows the meeting members to focus on solving one problem before attempting to take on the next and keeps confusion between competing subjects to a minimum.

2. Avoiding personal attacks during debates focuses the arguments on the subjects and not the personalities lauding those subjects. Personal attacks are distracting and misleading and can be used to camouflage negative issues by causing the conversation to be guided towards a personality (that has nothing to do with the issue) rather than the issue itself.

3. Limiting debates to the merit of the question prevents either side from using distractions to throw off the other or sway opinions. These kinds of distractions are also commonly referred to as "throwing red herrings". A Red Herring Fallacy is a kind of fallacy that is an irrelevant topic introduced in an argument to divert the attention of listeners or readers from the original issue. In literature, this

fallacy is often used in detective or suspense novels to mislead readers or characters or to induce them to make false conclusions. In arguments it is used to lead one side or the other down a false path to come to a false conclusion.

4. Dividing a complex question allows the MC to vote on parts of a question, to which they can agree to bring to a conclusion, while still allowing debate on the other part of the question.

Procedural Authority

Since most MCs and other smaller private societies don't have the need to write rules of order as extensively as a legislative body like the British Parliament or the U.S. Congress, they usually adopt the rules of a procedural authority. Arguably the most common procedural authority in use in the United States is *Robert's Rules of Order*.

Robert's Rules of Order

Generally, *"Robert's Rules of Order"* is a guide for conducting meetings and making decisions as a group. The purpose of the book is "to enable assemblies of any size, with due regard for every member's opinion, to arrive at the general will on the maximum number of questions of varying complexity in a minimum amount of time and under all kinds of internal climate ranging from total harmony to hardened or impassioned division of opinion." *"Robert's Rules of Order"* is designed for use in ordinary societies rather than legislative assemblies. The book states that it is "a codification of the present-day general parliamentary law". "General parliamentary law" refers to the common rules and customs for conducting business in organizations and assemblies which means it is about procedures for meetings and not about what is "legal" (i.e. it is not a law book). As a reference, it is designed to answer nearly any question of parliamentary procedure that may arise and was written so that organizations would not have to write extensive rules for themselves. In addition, members of different organizations could refer to the same book of rules. It is also important to know that if an MC has adopted a book of rules (such as Robert's Rules of Order) for conducting its meetings, it is still free to adopt its own rules which supersede any rules in the adopted book with which they conflict. Other than that, *"Robert's Rules of Order"* would apply.

Parliamentary Procedure Order of Business

The "order of business" is the established sequence in which business is taken up during church services. If the bylaws do not include a standard order of business, parliamentary procedure has established the following pattern after the Call to Order by the Sergeant-at-Arms:

- Rollcall
- Guest speakers
- Reading and approval of minutes
- Correspondence received
- Reports of directors, boards, and standing committees
- Reports of special committees
- Old business
  - Old business refers to questions that have carried over from the previous meeting as a result of that meeting having adjourned without completing its

order of business. The following items should be considered under old business:

- The question that was pending, when the previous meeting adjourned
- Any questions not reached at the previous meeting before adjournment
- Any questions postponed to the present meeting

- New business
  - o Following any old business, the Sergeant-at-Arms asks, "Is there any new business?" Full patch brothers in good standing can introduce new items of business or move to take from the, table any matter that is on the table.
- Comments for the good of the MC
  - o This step has a variation, "Passing the Gavel", which allows any full patch brother in good standing wishing to speak the opportunity to address the MC.
- Adjournment

Basic Parliamentary Procedure Definitions

Meeting—a meeting is called to order when a "quorum" is established.

Quorum—a quorum is the proportion of the members of an organization that must be present in order to conduct any business as defined in the bylaws. In the absence of a provision regarding a quorum, common law provides that a majority of members constitutes a quorum; however, your MC may have a specific definition of what a quorum is (i.e., 2/3^{rds} of the members of the MC). Once a quorum is present, the meeting and business may proceed. **Speaking**—when speaking to the MC no full patch brother in good standing may speak unless he has been recognized by the President, or Sergeant-at-Arms. Once granted the floor, a full patch brother in good standing should speak briefly, avoid repetition and confine all remarks to the topic at hand. If the speaking full patch brother does not follow these rules, he shall be called "out of order" and may be subject to interruption when a full patch brother would "rise to a point of order." Only a full patch brother in good standing may speak at a church service.

Parliamentary Procedure Voting Definitions

Voting—is normally done by voice, a show of hands or standing. If votes are to be recorded, a roll call may be taken. For elections, a ballot is required. The Sergeant-at-Arms is required to determine the "ayes" verses "nays" and assign the Assistant-Sergeant-at-Arms or conscript a full patch brother to be the "teller" to help count ballots. Only a full patch brother in good standing may vote in any election.

Majority—more than half the votes cast are required to pass a motion.

Two-thirds—Two out of every three full patch brothers in good standing voting on a motion is required to amend the by-laws, take up any matter out of its proper order of business, suspend rules, limit or close debate, discharge a committee, or refer reports back to a committee.

Unanimous—all full patch brothers in good standing voting on a motion must agree on a motion. Unanimous voting is rarely implemented because a single dissenter can prevent the vote from passing; therefore, it is reserved for extreme circumstances in most organizations. In the traditional MC; however, unanimous voting is used exclusively when voting prospects into the full patch brotherhood.

Breaking Ties—although the Sergeant-at-Arms may officiate church service, the President of the MC would be considered the chair for the purposes of parliamentary procedure. During church service the President never votes, unless his vote is needed to break a tie.

Main Motions—a motion for any group action may be made by a full patch brother in good standing who obtains the floor. Motions must be seconded by another full patch brother in good standing before the President or Sergeant-at-Arms calls for discussion.

Secondary Motions—a secondary motion can be made by full patch brother in good standing to alter the wording of a motion being discussed or to hasten/postpone a vote.

Suspension of the Rules—any full patch brother in good standing who obtains the floor may request a suspension of the rules to permit the group to do something ordinarily prohibited, such as permitting a guest speaker to speak out of the normal order of business. This requires a second, cannot be debated, and requires a 2/3^{rds} vote.

Appeal—if any full patch brother in good standing takes exception to any ruling by the President, he may "appeal the ruling of the Prez." An appeal requires a second, is debatable, and requires a majority vote to reverse the ruling.

Recess—any full patch brother in good standing who has the floor may request a short recess. When seconded, it may not be debated, and may be amended only as to the length of the recess. It requires a majority vote and if accepted, takes effect immediately. This motion takes precedence over all other motions except the motions to adjourn or to fix the time of adjournment.

Fix the Time to Adjourn—any full patch brother in good standing who has the floor may move to fix the time of adjournment. It requires a second, is not debatable, may be amended only as to the time of adjournment, and requires a majority vote. This motion takes precedence over all motions except that to adjourn.

Adjourn—any full patch brother in good standing who has the floor may move to adjourn. It requires a second, is not debatable, and requires a majority vote. It takes precedence over all other motions.

Case Study 1
Example of a Routine Church Service

Sergeant-at-Arms and designated prospects arrive at the clubhouse well before meeting time (at least 30 min) to ensure that:

- Tables and chairs are setup
- Gavel, bell, banners and other regalia are positioned and properly displayed
- Club's charter is present (always displayed in every meeting)
- Bylaws are present (always at hand in every meeting)
- Log book and sign in book are positioned (at every meeting)
- Sound system is working
- Lighting, temperature, ventilation are appropriate
- Audio-visual equipment is functioning
- Podium and guest speaking areas are appropriate
- Waiting area is prepped for individuals not privy to attend the entire meeting

- Assigns prospects or junior members to the door to greet full patch brothers
- Inspect uniforms of arriving brothers and collect colors at the door (some MCs require this step)
- Blows 5-minute warning whistle before meeting starts
- Introduction and thank you of guest speakers

After clubhouse has been prepared the Sergeant-at-Arms and prospects take up positions at the door and throughout the clubhouse to receive Officers and full patch brothers and usher them to their appropriate seating assignments. They receive guests and usher them to their appropriate waiting areas where they cannot hear or observe unauthorized portions of the Church service.

The Sergeant-at-Arms starts the meeting on time: At the time of the meeting, after receiving the nod of approval from the President, the Sergeant-at-Arms will dismiss the prospects to the appropriate waiting area and bring the meeting to order (perhaps with a ringing of the bell and by slamming down the gavel) and preceding to say;

"Hear Ye, Hear Ye, the 575th meeting of the Mighty Black Sabbath Motorcycle Club Nation Mother Chapter has come to order. Take your seats and maintain silence and respectability. You are required to show honor and respect to all full patch brothers and guests at all times. Disorderly conduct will not be tolerated and will be punished. You are under obligation to our bylaws. The truth will be spoken at all times. This meeting will utilize the communication standards of Parliamentary Procedure to wit Robert's Rules of Order will be recognized. With your permission, and if there are no objections, I humbly turn this meeting over to our duly elected President the

Honorable Black Dragon in service to our MC since 2009! Sir the meeting is yours!"

During Church the Sergeant-at-Arms will call out in sequence when certain activities should take place followed by a slam of his gavel:

- Prayer
- Roll call
- Financial Matters
- Old Business
- New Business
- Motions
- Discipline
- Arguments
- Fines
- Dues (also known as offerings)

The Sergeant-at-Arms will also:

- Handle late arrivals (including fining late brothers)
- Maintain order throughout meeting
- Excuse early departures (including fining early leavers)
- Preside over fines and disciplinary session

Induction of a new Prospect/Hang-arounds/Guests/ etc.

- Walks over and brings Prospect (guest, etc.) to podium
- Introduces Prospect and presents him to the MC (many MCs have all kinds of traditional ceremonies with this step)
- (Votes on hang-around into prospectship)
- Assigns or acknowledges Prospect's sponsor

Church comes to an End

- Conducts farewell to brothers

Judicial/Disciplinarian Board

Maintaining a balance of brotherhood and enforcing high standards is necessary for the brotherhood to stand the test of time and struggle. When a brother has committed an offense against the MC's bylaws he must face an accountability system competent to examine the merits of his case and come to a transparent adjudication and conclusion by his peers. An MC judicial board, also known as a committee hearing (among other terms), is used to handle these situations in a fair and consistent manner. The judicial board is a group of impartial brothers selected by the Sergeant-At-Arms to represent the brotherhood of the chapter and make decisions regarding member conduct. Examples where a judicial board might be utilized:

- A brother acts in a manner inconsistent with the high standards of the MC
- A brother breaks the bylaws
- A brother fails to pay dues
- A physical fight occurs between two brothers
- A physical fight occurs between two prospects
- A brother fails to make mandatory runs
- A brother steals from the MC or another brother
- A brother lies about another brother
- A brother screws the old-lady of another brother
- A brother speaks MC business outside the brotherhood
- A brother engages in cyber-banging

Note: *The Sergeant-at-Arms in some MCs conducts an investigation before any charges move forward. The best practices of handling charges and investigations can be found in many law reference books.*

Due Process 'a lesson in fairness!'

The term "Due Process" is described as a "fair treatment through the normal judicial system, especially as a citizen's entitlement."

WEX Legal Dictionary describes Due Process with, "The Fifth Amendment says to the federal government that no one shall be "deprived of life, liberty or property without due process of law." The Fourteenth Amendment, ratified in 1868, uses the same eleven words, called the 'Due Process Clause', to describe a legal obligation of all states."

Wikipedia describes Due Process as, "the legal requirement that the state must respect all legal rights that are owed to a person. Due process balances the power of law of the land and protects the individual person from it."

Law.com describes Due Process as, "a fundamental principle of fairness in all legal matters, both civil and criminal, especially in the courts."

The right of Due Process is a basic tenant in any democratically run society and has been thought of as essential for societal order and judicial fairness since the time of Plato and Socrates'. In a traditional MC any brother has the right to question the conduct of another brother or "Bring him up on charges". The Sergeant-at-Arms is responsible for ensuring that all brothers will be treated fairly and equally in accordance with the bylaws during all matters. This can be particularly hard when the Sergeant-at-Arms comes under the pressures of club politics, the interference of the President or other executive board members, the popularity of the accused (both positive and negative), bribery, collusion or other pressures designed to prevent fair treatment and due process, thereby eroding the purity of the MC. When faced with these difficult decisions know that no book can tell you what decisions to make. You are Sergeant-at-Arms! It is the responsibility of your position to do what is in the best interest of the MC, even if your decision costs you your position as Sergeant-at-Arms. My words of advice, if they mean anything to you, would be to always remember that YOU are the guardian of the MC's bylaws and it is upon you that its judicial system will succeed or fail. This means that you will not always, if ever, be popular. This can be a heavy burden for anyone, especially one who seeks popularity. Ask yourself, during any such trying times, "Am I capable of standing up to the task of fairness and impartiality no matter what my personal sacrifice may be?" If the answer is ever, "No," then you must recuse yourself and allow someone else to handle that responsibility.

The MC should consider Due Process as the established set of procedures the MC follows from the time the original action, accusation or issue arose, that resulted in charges , until the time a decision is made and sanctions (if any) are levied. This includes any charges, investigation, observance of rights, selection of the board, testimony, presentation of evidence, examination of witnesses, verdict, sentencing, appeals and final adjudication. The MC's bylaws will state what the Due Process is for the accused. The responsibility of the Sergeants-at-Arms is to carry out the bylaws exactly as outlined, without exception. If the bylaws are not fair work to change them!

Elements of Due Process or Fair Process
(As Commonly Recognized in the United States)

1997 Mary Rowe (https://ocw.mit.edu/courses/sloan-school-of-management/15-667-negotiation-and-conflict-management-spring-2001/lecture-notes/lec10_elements_due_process.pdf)

I. Due process may be seen as a matter of specific elements of process prescribed by various laws, statutes or policies, for example:

- Notice to the defendant; right to know the charges or all the major elements of the charges. In some cases the right to know the rules and policies that are relevant; in some cases the right to know who is the accuser;
- Timeliness of the process and of each step of the process;
- Right to present one's own evidence; in some cases the right to question the evidence brought by the other side; in some cases the right to face or meet with the accuser; the right to respond to the concerns that are raised;
- Right to accompaniment and someone to advise; in some cases the right to legal counsel;
- A fair and impartial fact-finding; a fair and impartial hearing;
- Right to a decision that is not capricious, unreasonable or arbitrary in nature;

- Notice of the decision; in some cases the right to a written decision with a statement of the reasons for the decision;
- In some cases the right to an appeals process;
- Freedom from retaliation, especially when raising a complaint in a responsible manner and in good faith;
- In some cases the right to have one's case treated the same way as similar cases;
- In some cases the right of privacy, as far as possible, for all concerned.

II. Due process may also be seen as "that which is due under the circumstances." Sometimes people use the term just to mean "the process I think I deserve" whether as a matter of law, employer policy, or just what the individual thinks is "fair."

****

Because of the considerable ambiguity of the term "Due Process," a prudent Sergeant-at-Arms may prefer the term "fairness"—speaking only of specific elements of procedure, rather than risk serious miscommunication. In particular, one does not wish to appear to have promised any specific element of procedure which the MC's bylaws does not necessarily guarantee, such as an open hearing or right of cross-examination.

Judicial Board Composition
In some MCs, the board must consist of full patch brothers in good standing who can make impartial decisions, with nothing to do with

the case. Seldom is the President allowed to sit on a judicial board as he could have a conflict of interest. In some MCs the board is made up of an odd number of 'jurors' because a brother must receive a majority vote to be found guilty and an odd number of 'jurors' ensures there can be no tie. Other MCs decide a tie as "not guilty" and therefore they allow an even number of brothers on the judicial board. It is not uncommon for the Sergeant-at-Arms to sit on the judicial board as a non-voting member, to ensure protocol and procedure are followed. He would only vote if there was a tie on an even number judicial board. There must be a strong attempt by the Sergeant-at-Arms to select a fair and impartial judicial board by selecting a broad spectrum of the MC's personalities and ranks. For example, one would not want to choose only officers, even if an officer is on trial. Brothers from the officer ranks as well as non-officers should be used in all trials. If possible, the Sergeant-at-Arms also avoid, choosing brothers from the same prospecting line. This could be seen as a conflict of interest and cause a club split along political lines.

Running a Judicial Board Hearing

The judicial board hearing can be either private—for only those involved in the proceeding, or open – for all full patch brothers in good standing, to attend, as specified in the MC bylaws. The parties should be given ample notice (24 hours at minimum or as specified in the bylaws). Once all of the members of the judicial board are present, they will elect a chair of the board and a secretary to take minutes. The Sergeant-at-Arms will serve as an ex-officio (non-voting) member and should make sure the meeting is run smoothly. Agenda for the hearing:

- Accusing brother states his case, presents his evidence and calls his witnesses allowing for the defending brother to cross-examine
- Defending brother defends his case, presents his evidence and calls his witnesses, allowing for the accusing brother to cross-examine
- Accusing brother presents closing arguments (no new evidence may be submitted)
- Defending brother presents closing arguments (no new evidence may be submitted)
- Both parties leave the room
- The judicial board discusses the case by re-examining the evidence and witness testimony as necessary
- The voting members decide if the accused member is guilty or innocent
- The voting members decide any penalty

Note: The judicial board members may ask either party questions during and after their cases are stated. The defending member should be made aware of all charges against him prior to the hearing (see previous Elements of Due Process or Fair Process section). Any additional witnesses may be brought in at the judicial board's discretion. Any witness testimony should be given before the defending brother states his case.

Conducting Suspension Proceedings

A full patch brother or prospect may be suspended from the MC for a variety of reasons, most of which are commonly listed in MC's bylaws. The Sergeant-at-Arms is responsible to ensure that the proper procedures according to the MC's traditions, protocols and bylaws are followed when suspending a brother. In some MC's bylaws the actual suspension procedures are listed. If not then here are some best practices that can be used to make the process as painless as possible:

- The suspended brother in question must be given written notice of the suspension at least 48 hours in advance, if not suspended at a judicial board hearing.
- Written notice must contain charges, time/place of the meeting location to turn in club items, section of the suspension procedures in the bylaws, a copy of the full Constitution and written directions to bring his active colors/cut to be confiscated by the Sergeant-at-Arms.

  Note: This can be a trying time for any suspended brother. The Sergeant-at-Arms must conduct this procedure with the respect, humility, compassion and understanding it deserves. For some people the MC is all they have. Losing their brotherhood, even for the time of a suspension can be a traumatic event. To handle this sensitive situation in any manner less than professional can result in disastrous consequences including injury or death. Be stern, but mature, professional and competent. Be the Sergeant-at-Arms.

- Within five (5) days after an expulsion, the MC must send a written suspension notice to the suspended brother's last known address and report the expulsion to the mother chapter, national executive board, or National President, whichever is more senior.

Conducting Expulsion Proceedings

A full patch brother or prospect may be expelled from the MC for a variety of reasons, most of which are commonly listed in MC's bylaws. The Sergeant-at-Arms is responsible to ensure that the proper procedures according to the MC's traditions, protocols and bylaws are followed when expelling a brother. In some MC's bylaws the actual expulsion procedures are listed. If not here are some best practices that can be used to make the process as painless as possible:

- A quorum of voting members of the chapter must be present to expel a brother (in some MC's it takes a unanimous vote instead of a quorum).
- The brother in question must be given written notice of the expulsion at least 48 hours in advance.
- Written notice must contain charges, time/place of the hearing, section of the expulsion proceedings, and a copy of the full Constitution and written direction to return all club related materials, including patches, mugs, shirts, t-shirts, vests, cuts, hats, business cards —anything that contains the MC's logo.
- The accused brother must be given the opportunity to present a defense to the voting chapter brothers.
- At least 2/3^{rds} of present voting members must vote in favor of the expulsion for it to pass (depending on the bylaws).
- If the accused brother is voted out and expelled the Sergeant-at-Arms will collect the MC's belongings and separate the MC's patch from his vest or cut.

> **Note:** *This can be a trying time for any former brother. The Sergeant-at-Arms must conduct this procedure with the respect, humility, compassion and understanding is deserves. For some people the MC is all they have. Losing their brotherhood can be a traumatic event. To handle this sensitive situation in any manner less than professional can result in disastrous consequences including injury or death. Be stern, but mature, professional and competent. Be the Sergeant-at-Arms.*

- Within five (5) days after an expulsion, the MC must send a written expulsion notice to the expelled brother's last known address and report the expulsion to the mother chapter, national executive board, or National President, whichever is more senior.
- The expelled former brother will have thirty (30) days to present evidence that club tattoos have been removed by laser, burned off, cut off, or covered with another tattoo.

Case Study 2:
A Sample Case Involving Due Process

1. Within the statute of limitations, stated in the bylaws, an incident occurs and a brother submits charges, in writing, to the Sergeant-at-Arms for a judicial hearing, including the details of the incident.
2. The Sergeant-at-Arms examines the complaint and conducts an investigation and determines there is sufficient evidence to proceed.

3. The Sergeant-at-Arms makes a recommendation to the Executive Board that a judicial board or committee hearing should be held.

4. Upon receiving the go-ahead from the executive board the Sergeant-at-Arms selects the judicial board members and chooses a time for a hearing, notifying the accused member of the charges and the hearing in an advance time according to the bylaws.

5. The parties are brought before the judicial board and the accusation and evidence are presented. The accused brother is given the opportunity to defend himself, present opposing evidence, call witnesses and question his accuser(s). The judicial board has the opportunity to question both parties and witnesses.

6. The judicial board has a closed discussion and makes a decision by taking a vote according to the bylaws.

7. If found guilty the accused brother may submit a written appeal of the judicial board's decision to the executive board within the time allotted by the MC's bylaws.

8. If the guilty verdict is upheld the guilty brother may appeal the decision to the full chapter, presented in writing to the President within the time allotted by the bylaws.

9. Chapter vote by the full body; decision is final.

CHAPTER 5:
CONFLICT RESOLUTION:
NEGOTIATION & MEDIATION

Conflicts and Disagreements

Whenever people are together, in any setting, there will be conflicts and disagreements that arise between them. Resolving these challenges quickly is important to maintaining good discipline, order and morale within the MC. The Sergeant-at-Arms may be called upon to resolve many conflicts afflicting the MC. Conflicts between brothers can cause club splits and conflicts between rival MCs can result in club wars. To obtain a firm knowledge of conflict resolution skills one must develop themselves in the areas of negotiation and mediation strategies. Knowing how to effectively solve issues between warring parties will be the key to ending a conflict with an agreement that works for everyone.

Negotiation

Negotiation is a method used by people to settle differences among themselves without the use of a third party. It is a process by which compromise or agreement is reached while avoiding argument and dispute. For negotiations to be successful parties will have to be fair and seek mutually beneficial solutions that maintain relationships, even though they are trying to achieve the best possible outcome for their position. An example of using negotiation to solve a conflict is when two brothers are locked in an argument and the Sergeant-at-Arms forces them to sit down and forge an agreement between themselves. He should give them guidance using the following set of standards:

Why Negotiate?

Because it is inevitable that conflict will arise when people find themselves together and when it does there has to be a way of solving disagreements such that the MC will remain intact and continue to thrive, whether that conflict is from within the MC or without.

Stages of Negotiation

There are many ways to achieve a successful negotiation. However it is accomplished best if the steps are structured. Here is one example:

1. Preparation
2. Discussion
3. Goal setting
4. Negotiate
5. Agreement
6. Implementation

Preparation

Prepare all sides for the meeting by setting the date and time as well as the time limit for the meeting. Gather a solid investigation of the facts. If the negotiation is between brothers in the MC research should be done on the section of the MC's bylaws that pertain to the situation.

Discussion

In the discussion stage each side simply presents their case from their point of view only. There is no argument in this stage, or any back and forth. In this way everyone knows solidly where each side is coming from. Notes should be taken to refer back to during the negotiation stage.

Goal Setting

After all sides have been heard during the negotiation stage then goals can be set that each side would like to achieve. Look for common ground in goal setting because during the negotiation stage it will be easier to achieve agreements in those areas first. They can also be icebreakers in getting all sides to agree on the stickier issues when they believe they have already made some gains.

Negotiate

Focus on obtaining a win-win solution. If everyone feels they are benefitting from the negotiation, in some way, it is easier to move them towards the agreement. Remember that compromise allows each side to walk away from the negotiation with a win which is good. Even though one might not get everything, getting some things can be better than getting nothing.

Agreement

After the negotiation has established, as well as, all points of view, and what each party can accept, then an agreement can be reached. If all sides accept the agreement, either verbally, or in writing, then the resolution has almost been achieved. It can be difficult to get people to actually accept an agreement as it should mean a cessation to the conflict. Lots of folks like to still engage in conflict even after the battle is over. The Sergeant-at-Arms should remind all to keep an open mind and to be willing to accept the agreement, in good faith, once it has been issued.

Implementation

A course of action completes the agreement, so once implemented the agreement has been seen through to fruition and the conflict is then resolved through successful negotiation.

Failure to Agree

When the negotiation process breaks down then it has failed. The next step could be to schedule another meeting to negotiate again. The same process can be repeated again and again, if the parties believe that an agreement can eventually be reached.

When Negotiation Fails

When negotiation fails the Sergeant-at-Arms can move to another phase of conflict resolution known as mediation.

Mediation

Mediation differs from negotiation because it involves using an impartial third party to help those in a conflict come to a resolution. A mediator can help solve conflicts that have gone beyond the negotiation stage. In the mediation stage the mediator does not make decisions for the parties involved. Instead he helps the parties work together to develop their own agreement.

Stages of Mediation

There are many ways to achieve a successful mediation. However it is accomplished best if the steps are structured. Here is one example:

1. Preparation
2. Defining the Conflict
3. Defining Points of Agreement

4. Creating Options for Agreement
5. Developing an Agreement

Preparation

Apart from setting up the place and time and possibly the length of the meeting ground rules for how the mediation will be run should also be established. For instance, only one person can speak at a time, no verbal abuse at any time, when one person is talking all others will listen in silence, no yelling, no cutting off, and also fines may be established for anyone violating the ground rules. For instance a $25.00 fine could be issued every time someone speaks out of turn. Also ensure that all parties will know that the mediator is impartial. This is one of the reasons the Sergeant-at-Arms stays out of MC politics so that he will always be seen as impartial when he has to mediate between two factions within the MC.

Defining the Conflict

The mediator listens to all sides of the story. This can be done combined or individually. Also the mediator must clarify what each side wants to accomplish.

Defining Points of Agreement

The mediator helps the parties to understand each other's points of view. A focus on the future instead of the past should be suggested. The mediator can summarize points of conflict in neutral terms and help parties see terms of mutual agreement.

Creating Options for Agreement

The mediator should look towards getting the parties to agree in the easiest areas first. These small victories can be icebreakers towards moving to the more complex remaining problems. Nothing like starting with a win or two.

Developing an Agreement
Agreements should be SMART:

- Specific
- Measurable
- Attainable
- Realistic
- Time-bound

Note: A mediator must be non-biased and most never appear to take sides. He must acknowledge points made by both sides and spend equal time with each side.

CHAPTER 6: ADMINISTRATIVE TASKS

Goal Setting

An effective Sergeant-at-Arms will excel at being able to set goals and achieve milestones towards reaching those goals. A goal is the result or achievement toward a directed effort. Milestones are the metrics or steps of achievement accomplished to reaching that goal.

For instance, if one didn't like the over-all lack of knowledge the brothers displayed when asked questions about the MC's history they could set a goal to improve the brothers' knowledge of the MC's history to a minimum basic level that would be acceptable to all. To go about setting milestones to achieve this goal one could write out a plan like this:

1. **Goal** = raise club history knowledge to basic level among 95% of brothers.
2. **Milestone 1** = poll executive board to obtain acceptable minimum standards of club history (x number of questions).
3. **Milestone 2** = Develop and pass out study sheets containing those questions and answers to all brothers.
4. **Milestone 3** = Develop a memory game and pass out cue cards to all brothers with answers
5. **Milestone 4** = Teach brothers memory game and give awards to brothers who are playing the game during leisure time in the MC
6. **Milestone 5** = Give test to all brothers and measure outcome

7. **Question:** Did 95% of brothers pass the test with an acceptable score? Yes? Milestone accomplished and goal reached. No? Re-evaluate the program, assign new milestones (if necessary) re-implement the program.

One can set goals and milestones for any project they wanted to accomplish within the MC, from getting brothers to ride more often, to getting brothers to all wear the correct uniform without uniform violations. When setting goals for any project, one should always determine the metrics that can be used to appropriately determine success or failure.

Planning and Scheduling

It is written that "failing to plan is planning to fail." A successful Sergeant-at-Arms will excel at planning and meeting schedules. This goes along with goal setting discussed previously.

Improvement

A successful Sergeant-at-Arms is always on the scout for ways to improve the MC. For example, it could be improving the physical security of the clubhouse. If the Sergeant-at-Arms notices that too much loitering in the parking lot of the clubhouse is causing fights to break out between visiting MCs and neighborhood civilians (which could jeopardize the MC's ability to renew its lease in the future), he should take action to improve parking lot security and eliminates loitering—thus avoiding future conflicts that would not be good for the MC. Continuous improvement of processes makes the difference between a successful Sergeant-at-Arms and an unsuccessful one.

Budgets and Cost Control

Successful management of club monies is the cornerstone of a successful brotherhood. Since the Sergeant-at-Arms is responsible for physical security of the MC clubhouse he is often also responsible for the operational fitness of the clubhouse. Lights bulbs, toilet tissue, wax, mops, buckets, cleaning supplies, computer supplies, coin wrappers, cash-register paper, the list goes on. The Sergeant-at-Arms' budget should cut costs and control waste and abuse.

Clubhouse Maintenance

If the Sergeant-at-Arms is responsible for the clubhouse he will be responsible for its maintenance and upkeep. He will assign cleaning and repair tasks to prospects, hang-arounds and/or brothers. If there is a building manager the Sergeant-at-Arms will oversee him, as the maintenance and orderly operation of the MC is vital to the club's security.

Communicating

The Sergeant-at-Arms has far too much going on to be a poor communicator. Most of his job will consist of getting others to make things happen and report back to him when the job is completed successfully or come to him for additional support if there are challenges. He must master the art of speaking positively to people to encourage support, rather than negatively speaking to brothers in a way that is considered to be "down-talking" or "arrogant." This is the quickest way NOT to get things done. The Sergeant-at-Arms must always remember that brothers VOLUNTEER their time to the MC. They are not receiving a paycheck. He cannot speak to grown men as though they are his employees, slaves or servants! The brothers will turn on him quickly if he thinks this is okay. He must realize that they follow because they love the MC not because they have to follow. Compel them through effective communication. Leave the hollering and screaming, cursing and belittling at home.

Training

The successful Sergeant-at-Arms will meet his immense training duties. When not assigning tasks, running the accountability system, handing out fines, or improving MC security, he needs to be training members and overseeing the proper training of prospects. Some of the subjects he may provide instruction for:

- Clubhouse security
- Properly escorting abusive guest(s) out of the building
- Checking visitors for weapons
- MC bylaws and protocol
- Set protocol and visiting other MC's clubhouses
- Uniform rules
- Elections procedures

Safety

Safety on the road is the responsibility of the Road Captain and the President. Safety on the Set, in the clubhouse, at rallies and field meets is the responsibility of the Sergeant-at-Arms. Safety briefs when the MC is about to go on outings is a must. The Sergeant-at-Arms is responsible for knowing the temperature of the MC Set. He knows where tensions on the Set exist, what MC is at war with another, where law enforcement is cracking down on bikers, and the details of a myriad of other safety concerns. He will continually keep his brothers advised with up-to-date safety information.

Working Conditions

The Sergeant-at-Arms is responsible for the working conditions under which the brothers, prospects, hang-arounds, and supporters in his charge will toil. When the need for working parties around the clubhouse arises the Sergeant-at-Arms will ensure safe conditions, good working pace, safety precautions, and fair distribution of work. He will also keep down hazing and verbal abuse among members of the work detail. If they are ever placed in a dangerous situation it is the Sergeant-Soldier's responsibility to ensure that they are removed from harm's way.

Special Considerations with Women in the MC

A MC brotherhood is a private, male-dominated organization and most MCs feel they can do whatever they want where women are concerned, but there are still ways that the MC can get into trouble when dealing with women incorrectly. It is accepted in most traditional MCs that women may have minor roles in MC culture. Still, as more women are riding, starting clubs, mingling in the clubhouses and joining the support ranks, the Sergeant-at-Arms will have ever increasing responsibilities to supervise and protect these women. Whether the MC has properties, a social club, a support club or otherwise, when women are a part of the social makeup of the MC they are part of the Sergeant-at-Arms' responsibility. There are a myriad of challenges associated with dealing with women in the MC. The Sergeant-at-Arms should be calm, resolute and professional.

Sexual Harassment

Sexual harassment, rape, and date-rape are real problems in any society. MC brotherhoods are no exception. Just because an MC is wild and unruly its brothers should not falsely believe that they can't be sued, charged or put in prison for breaking the law. If a MC is coed its members should really think through the issues that can occur when men and women come together in a social structure and develop policies accordingly.

The Sergeant-at-Arms should advise the MC to be very careful when hiring employees outside the MC to work MC events. Having employees on a payroll (either on the books or under the table) requires an awareness among the brothers that the brotherhood is responsible for providing a safe and professional working environment. Brothers should be advised to keep their jeers, whistles, unwanted sexual comments, and innuendos to themselves. To act otherwise could get the MC in legal hot water. And yes, men can sue men for sexual harassment as well. For example, a drunken brother calling a male employee a [fagg*t], while that employee is on the job could land the MC in court settling a case with plenty of dollar bills in hand.

Sexual harassment is generally defined as unwelcome sexual advances, requests for sexual favors or any other verbal or physical conduct of a sexual nature when either:

- The conduct is made as a term or condition of an individual's employment, education, living environment or participation in the MC.
- The acceptance or refusal of such conduct is used as the basis or a factor in decisions affecting and individual's employment, environment or participation in the MC.

Sexual harassment is defined by law and includes requests for sexual favors, sexual advances or other sexual conduct when

(1) submission is either explicitly or implicitly a condition affecting certain decisions;

(2) the behavior is sufficiently severe or pervasive as to create an intimidating, hostile or repugnant environment; or

(3) the behavior persists despite objection by the person to whom the conduct is directed

Types of Sexual Harassment

Generally speaking, there are two types of sexual harassment:

- *"quid pro quo"*
- *hostile environment*

Quid pro quo means "this for that". Sexual harassment occurs when it is stated or implied that an inner club or employment decision about a member, prospect, property, hang-around, or employee depends upon whether they submit to conduct of a sexual nature. Quid pro quo sexual harassment also occurs when it is stated or implied that an individual must submit to conduct of a sexual nature in order to participate in an MC activity or be employed by the MC. So, for example, if a stripper is made to believe that she is likely to get a job stripping in the clubhouse on bike nights if she goes on a date with the club's President, or agrees to go in the back room to "demonstrate" how badly she wants the job, the stripper is possibly being subjected to "quid pro quo" sexual harassment. It's also sexual harassment to suggest to her that she might get a raise or get to keep more of her tips if she performs some sexual act or agrees to date a member of the MC.

Hostile environment sexual harassment occurs when unwelcome conduct of a sexual nature creates an intimidating, threatening or abusive working or club environment or is so severe, persistent or pervasive that it affects a person's ability to participate in or benefit from an MC activity. While a person engaging in harassing behavior most often has some form of power or authority over the person being harassed, that is not always the case. The harasser can be a peer of the person being harassed. Sometimes the harasser is harassing a person who has power over them. For example, a supervisee can sexually harass a supervisor.

More Examples of Sexual Harassment

- *Unwanted sexual statements:* Sexual or "dirty" jokes, comments on physical attributes, spreading rumors about or rating others as to sexual activity or performance, talking about one's sexual activity in front of others and displaying or distributing sexually explicit drawings, pictures and/or written material. Unwanted sexual statements can be made in person, in writing, electronically (email, instant messaging, blogs, web pages, etc.) and otherwise.

- *Unwanted personal attention:* Letters, telephone calls, visits, pressure for sexual favors, pressure for unnecessary personal interaction and pressure for dates where a sexual/romantic intent appears evident but remains unwanted.

- *Unwanted physical or sexual advances:* Touching, hugging, kissing, fondling, touching oneself sexually for others to view, sexual assault, intercourse or any other sexual activity.

MC's Sexual Harassment Policy

It is important to know that members of a private society can still be held criminally or civilly liable in a court of law if a crime has been committed. The Sergeant-at-Arms should help his MC decide what its policy is going to be towards sexual harassment and then does not allow the brotherhood to stray from it. Having a weak policy or no policy at all could get the MC the kind of media coverage and law enforcement attention no one wants.

Discrimination Policy

Many MCs discriminate on the basis of race (potential members are barred from joining by their race) and most traditional MC's discriminate on the basis of sex (women are not allowed to join because of their sex) so there may not ever be an anti-discrimination policy when it comes to the inclusion of members into any particular MC's private society. But if an MC is hiring employees to work for it then it must follow the employment laws regardless of the racial makeup of its membership. If one's MC does want to have an anti-discrimination policy it can use elements of *"Title VII of the Civil Rights Act of 1964"* to base its policy. *"Title VII of the Civil Rights Act of 1964"* prohibits discrimination against an employee or applicant for employment on the basis of race, color, religion, sex, or national origin, and against a broad range of employment practices.

Evaluation of Brothers

As the enforcer of the MC's accountability system it may be necessary for the Sergeant-at-Arms to issue punishments, fines or other disciplinary sanctions while performing his duties. He may also have to make recommendations as to whether a brother should be suspended or separated from the MC for missing runs, violating bylaws, fighting or lack of participation. Morale can suffer when brothers see that others are not pulling their weight or are missing from functions they should be riding to, or have poor attitudes about the MC's overall business. An aware Sergeant-at-Arms should be the one to recommend a judicial board against a brother.

The Sergeant-at-Arms should develop a good evaluation process that allows keeps him abreast as to who is doing what in the MC and if their participation is valuable. He should document who is continually breaking rules, getting fines and refusing to participate. This documented evidence will be invaluable when it comes time to make decisions as to the futures of errant club brothers in potential judicial proceedings.

Electronic Data Processing and Social Media

Today's Sergeant-at-Arms will be vitally ill-equipped if he does not embrace technology and today's standards of communication. MCs, if they are to survive, will be getting younger, not the other way around. If the Sergeant-at-Arms refuses to engage in social media, and any emerging communication technology that will power tomorrow's modalities, he is already behind the times. Issues will come up, for which he will not be aware and cannot put a handle on before things get out of hand, simply because he is not in the current communication loop for the MC. For instance, how can he stop cyber-banging (club fighting on social media) if he has no ability to monitor social media because he has no social media accounts? He won't be able to monitor the MC's social media accounts, email, websites, group chats and other portals, where threats to the MC could arise, if he refuses to embrace the technology 90% of the club is using. Hearing old-school senior club officers proudly exclaim how they have no connectivity to modern cell phones, tablets, or social media accounts and never plan to get any, is an indication that they are out of touch and disconnected from the true heartbeat of today's modern MC.

Motivation of Members

To motivate brothers the Sergeant-at-Arms must learn how to engage and uplift them. He must challenge their imaginations and be an example that will make them want to reach higher and accomplish more. The Sergeant-at-Arms must be tough but he shouldn't become an intolerable bully. Some of the most basic ideas of motivation of men to excel is to praise them in public and criticize them in private. Don't neglect to tell them "I'm proud of you" and "Job well done." These phrases go much further in motivating brothers then cursing them out and belittling them.

Maintaining Tradition, Regalia, and Rituals

Maintaining traditions, regalia and rituals is an important but often-overlooked duty of the Sergeant-at-Arms. The MC's observation of rituals is the glue that binds the brothers together and makes the MC family different from all others.

- Rituals could be a pledge of allegiance, a slogan or an initiation.
- Tradition could be a ride the MC commonly takes that it has taken from the beginning of the MC's birth, how a brother is awarded a patch, certificate of completion, or the way brothers behave at funerals.

- Regalia could be the specific way the cut is worn during ceremonies, dress blues, or how an honorary symbol is worn when a brother passes, or perhaps something that is worn when a brother or founder dies.

No matter whether he is admonishing members for putting extra patches on their back, when the MC's policy states that nothing should be placed on the back of the cut but the MC's patch, chastising a brother for losing his cut or reprimanding a brother for allowing his lady to burn it up, it is up to the Sergeant-at-Arms to enforce the standards of the code of dress outlined in the bylaws.

Writing a Budget for Sergeant-at-Arms Office

Every office needs a budget to run efficiently. Within the MC there should be a budgeting system that appropriates funds for necessities of office. The best way to get what is needed in a timely manner is to have an established budget written and presented to the executive board. This ensures that the funds are allocated and available when required.

When setting the budget for Sergeant-at-Arms one must take into consideration all of the possible expenses that may be incurred by the Sergeant-at-Arms Department, then work with the treasurer to allocate the correct amount of the budget. Part of the list will come from the goal setting, planning and scheduling stages talked about earlier in this chapter. The Sergeant-at-Arms has three major areas of responsibility to consider:

- Budget for administration
  - Patches
  - Church meetings supplies

- o   Ballots and elections materials
- o   Flags, banners for runs and field meets
- o   Decals for bikes and chase vehicles
- Budget for security
  - o   Clubhouse security
  - o   Annuals and parties
  - o   Presidential escort security
  - o   Security on the MC Set
  - o   Security on runs and field meets
- Budget for Clubhouse
  - o   Cleaning supplies
  - o   Paint and Maintenance supplies
  - o   Restroom supplies
  - o   Bar stocking supplies
  - o   Liquor Cabinet/Alcohol/Beer
  - o   Ash trays, trash cans, etc.
  - o   Kitchen supplies/oil/pots, pans etc.

The list of expenses may look something like this:

- Name Patches (100 on hand)
- Back Patches (25 on hand)
- Church Supplies
- Flags, Gavels,
- Metal Detector Wand
- Flash Lights
- Walkie Talkies
- Security Shirts
- Night Sticks
- Parking Cones

Budget Request Form

The Sergeant-at-Arms could use a budget request form that would list all expenses projected for the month, quarter or year, for approval to the board:

SERGEANT AT ARMS BUDGET	REQUEST FORM
NAME PATCHES	$ 200.00
BACK PATCHES	$2000.00
CHURCH SERVICES SUPPLIES	$ 500.00
FLAGS, GAVEL, CEREMONIAL	$ 350.00
METAL DETECTOR WAND	$ 150.00
FLASH LIGHTS (CLUBS)	$ 500.00
WALKIE TALKIES 30	$ 900.00
TOTAL REQUEST AMOUNT	$4600.00

Once submitted and approved, the budget is now set to enable accomplishment of the goals set for Sergeant-at-Arms.

CHAPTER 7:
THE CLUBHOUSE

The Sergeant-at-Arms is responsible for the clubhouse and grounds. Keeping the clubhouse established and running in the neighborhood is sometimes the biggest battle the MC will have concerning the clubhouse. It is the Sergeant-at-Arms responsibility to keep all brothers on point regarding that issue and to work with the President to keep community relations in order.

Duty Roster

The Sergeant-at-Arms writes the duty roster. The duty roster is the schedule of brothers and prospects that will have club duty. Club duty can be defined as everything from working the bar on bike nights to controlling entry at the door. It lists the time for check-in and departure. It is ultimately the Sergeant-at-Arms responsibility to ensure someone is on duty at all appropriate times. The duty roster is normally written for 1 to 2 month intervals. The Sergeant-at-Arms typically provides the brothers a certain amount of time to turn in their duty requests or limitations a week or two before he writes the roster. In some MCs once the roster is written the member is responsible for providing his own replacement.

Check-in Log

The Sergeant-at-Arms is responsible for maintaining the duty check-in log. The check-in log is signed in by the senior brother who takes the duty for the night. This log is provides an account for supplies, monies, register receipts, etc., that are checked out (and then checked in when returned) for the duty. Things that might be on the check-in log:

- Cash amount necessary to back the bar
- Amount of alcohol being checked out
- Supplies necessary to run club house
- Walkie talkies, security wands and other equipment

Field Day

The Sergeant-at-Arms is responsible for assigning prospects and brothers to clubhouse cleaning details. In the US Navy, cleanup is referred to as "Field Day". Routine clubhouse Field Day is performed by the off-going duty crew.

Parking Lot and Building Exterior Cleaning

The Sergeant-at-Arms is responsible for the upkeep of the grounds and parking lot surrounding the MC clubhouse. He will assign prospects and brothers to maintain, cleanup and paint where necessary. He will also assign mowing duties, as necessary, to keep the grounds looking smart. Pride in ownership can ensure confidence with any neighbors suspicious or hostile towards the existence of the MC.

Neighboring Structures and Parking Lots

The motorcycle clubhouse can be a wild place where "boys will be boys'. A good way to turn neighboring businesses against the MC is for proprietors to show up to work at their businesses Monday morning to find beer bottles, used condoms, cigarette butts and other party materials littering their parking lots after the MC has been partying all weekend. Neighboring yards can also become the target of these discarded items. As part of his duties, the Sergeant-at-Arms ensures neighboring properties are policed and cleaned of club refuse after parties and bike nights.

Bar Stocking

The Sergeant-at-Arms may be responsible for stocking the bar and keeping the liquor count and the liquor storage locked until it is to be used. Appropriate receipts and logs should be used to keep track of these items.

Bar Equipment and Cleanliness

The Sergeant-at-Arms is responsible for ensuring that all bar and drink dispensing equipment is in good working order. He will also make sure that all cleanliness standards meet or exceed local ordinances necessary to provide safe consumables to bar patrons.

Kitchen Equipment and Cleanliness

The Sergeant-at-Arms is responsible for ensuring that all kitchen and food cooking and dispensing equipment is in good working order. He will also make sure that all cleanliness standards meet or exceed local ordinances necessary to provide safe consumables to club kitchen patrons.

Candy Machines and Soda Machines

The Sergeant-at-Arms may be responsible for ensuring that the club's vending machines are stocked and in good working order. Whereas the Secretary or Treasurer may be responsible for collecting the money from the machines, the Sergeant-at-Arms is responsible for making sure that everything in the MC is operational and in adequate supply.

DJ Equipment

The Sergeant-at-Arms will ensure that the MC's entertainment systems are well maintained and in good working order. He will account for club microphones, speakers, disco-lighting, spot lights, karaoke machines and other club equipment and make sure that the equipment is secured and locked up after use. This equipment may also be on the check-in log assigned to brothers who have daily or weekly duty.

Environment and Thermostats

The Sergeant-at-Arms is responsible for the temperature and thermostats in the clubhouse. Club brothers should consult with him before adjusting the thermostats and turning heating and air-conditioning units on and off, since the Sergeant-at-Arms may have a specific budget he must adhere to concerning the environmental condition of the MC.

Lost and Found

The Sergeant-at-Arms is responsible for the MC's lost and found. There is nothing more gratifying than to have one's cell phone or wallet returned when it is lost at a clubhouse. It goes a long way in securing returning visits from patrons.

Once, in the early 1980s, a lady lost her wallet at the Black Sabbath MC mother chapter. It contained all of her rent money. When the Sergeant-at-Arms returned her wallet with every dollar accounted for, she was so elated she retold that story for the next 20 years.

CHAPTER 8:
SERGEANT-AT-ARMS AND PROSPECTS

The Sergeant-at-Arms is one of the most revered figures a prospect will ever know. The Soldier-Sergeant is the backbone of the MC. He is the security, the keeper of order and the protector of the weak. Since prospects are the lowest rank in the MC, they are the weakest group with the smallest voice. Consequently they are rife for exploitation. Ultimately, beyond their sponsors, they will look to the Sergeant-at-Arms for guidance and protection in all things.

Guiding the Prospect Sponsors

The Sergeant-at-Arms ensures prospect sponsors are responsible for the proper training and conduct of the prospects they sponsor. He ensures that the prospects speak through their sponsors for all concerns and follow-up to make sure those concerns are addressed by the sponsors. If a sponsor does not adequately protect, train and educate a prospect, it is not only a failure of the sponsor, it is also a failure of the Sergeant-at-Arms! Although discipline issues of prospects are routinely handled by the prospect's sponsor, the Sergeant-at-Arms will oversee this discipline and ensure that it falls within the specifications and expectations of the MC's bylaws. The Sergeant-at-Arms may oversee the prospect sponsors to ensure their training methods are appropriate and that their prospects are receiving at least the basic level of education the brotherhood expects. He may charge, fine and even suspend prospect sponsors who are not performing their sponsorship duties satisfactorily according the MC's bylaws. The Sergeant-at-Arms may also recommend prospect sponsors be removed from their duties for poor performance.

Club Hazing of Prospects

A traditional MC will be more concerned about creating a learning environment where prospects learn what it takes to become valued brothers rather than humiliating prospective members through emasculation and hazing. Still, as long as there are full patch brothers and prospects in an MC you will always find some level of hazing. It is the Sergeant-at-Arms' duty to monitor, regulate and limit this hazing, keeping in mind the temperament and tolerance of the prospect being hazed. He will also fine or suspend overly zealous members who violate bylaws or create an unsafe, unhealthy, sexually harassing, humiliating, intimidating or illegal environments for prospective members that may discredit the MC due to violence, injury, mental/emotional distress or death to a prospective member. The Sergeant-at-Arms must NEVER participate in any hazing events of prospective members. To do so is a conflict of interest to the Sergeant-at-Arms' ability to discipline members for overstepping their bounds. If a brother can say, "You did it to", the Sergeant-at-Arms will lose his credibility in awarding disciplinary action to rule breakers. The Sergeant-at-Arms will remember his commitment to protecting even the weakest and lowest ranking of all the brothers and prospective brothers of the MC. If he cannot protect them who will?

Hazing of Prospects by Other MCs

The Sergeant-at-Arms will ensure that the MC's prospects understand that at no time will they be hazed or intimidated by outside MCs. The MC's prospects are prospects for this MC alone and no one else.

CHAPTER 9:
INJURIES, DEATHS, AND FUNERALS

It has been said that you can "measure how civilized a society is by how it treats its dead". Motorcycle clubs are highly respected private societies because ceremony, dignity and traditions are recognized when handling the remains of fallen brothers and conducting their funerals. The Sergeant-at-Arms ensures the MC handles the deaths and funerals of brothers respectfully, appropriately, honorably and according to the bylaws.

Media Black Outs During Emergencies

It is the important that information about a brother's injuries or death is not made public until the appropriate time. There are times when the MC will learn about a member's death before the family, such as when a brother expires on the road due to a motorcycle fatality while riding in the pack. In this case, the Sergeant-at-Arms should instruct brothers to remain silent and enforce a media and social media blackout upon the MC until such time as the blackout is lifted by the President or his designated affiliate such as the Public Relations Officer (PRO). Family members shouldn't learn of their loved one's demise over social media or by seeing pictures of an accident scene posted in a chat room.

Notifications of Next of Kin

The Sergeant-at-Arms should prevent members from making phone calls and sending texts, etc. to notify next of kin of any emergency concerning club brothers. The President is the spokesman for the MC and should be the only one contacting next of kin on behalf of the MC.

Support at Hospitals

Brothers will want to show up at the hospital to show respect and support for the downed brother. This can be a trying time. Often the blood-family can hate the downed brother's involvement with the MC and attempt to use the tragedy to exact revenge on the MC family. The blood-family, in a fit of jealousy or hatred, could bar brothers from the hospital and instruct hospital staff not to give out information or provide access to their family member (your fallen club brother). It is not uncommon for the family to blame the MC – especially if the brother was injured or killed during a MC event or while racing his bike, riding with the brotherhood, or worse yet, beefing on behalf of the MC. This is a time to remember that the blood-family has all legal and moral rights according to the law and society in general—even if they had nothing to do with the brother while he was alive! If the MC is allowed to participate it should be there. If not it is good for the Sergeant-at-Arms to remind brothers that funerals are for the living. If the brothers were good to him while he was alive then he died knowing where he stood in their hearts. An MC fighting with a blood-family at a hospital or during a funeral is never a good look for the MC. Regardless of the situation the MC must be good to the blood-family. Within a few days, after processing their loss, the blood-family will often change their minds and allow the MC-family to join them. Remember the MC-family is grieving over a brother it has known for some time. The blood-family is grieving over a family member they've known a lifetime. Professional behavior of the MC goes a long way in demonstrating to the blood-family that a brother's participation in the extended family was worth his time, effort, devotion, dedication and love.

The other part about visiting and supporting a member in the hospital is that it can take a hell of a toll on the MC, especially if that brother is going to be down for quite some time (weeks, months or years). Remember that support during a crisis should continue long after the crisis is over. There may be a recovery period and a need for rehabilitation to re-learn basic skills like how to walk or talk, as well as processing the psychological toll the incident may have exacted. The MC will have a long road supporting their brother. The Sergeant-at-Arms can take control of this kind of chaotic period:

- Put the brothers on a watch routine spreading the duties evenly and ensuring coverage 24/7, weekly or monthly coverage
- Assign a club ombudsman to the family to be with them, assist them, or answer any questions they may have of the MC
- Assign a watch bill for the long term recovery so that there will be club brothers involved for the entire recovery period and not just for the short term

Thinking through the sad times is challenging. One should be wise and forward thinking, constructive and supportive.

Military Guard

If a deceased brother was active or prior military his family may request a military guard. Avoid the temptation of competing with the military guard for attention. The MC-family is burying a brother and so is the military-family. Allow the young men and women to do their jobs with respect and professionalism. They have a routine they follow at every funeral. Don't get in their way. They will make way for the MC as well. They will play taps, give a gun salute, present the wife and or mother with a flag and then be on their way. They may have several more funerals to attend that day. They won't have time for monkey business.

Patriot Guard

These are the best bikers in the world! If a brother was active or prior military the MC will truly be blessed to have the Patriot Guard involved. The way they take care of active and prior military funerals is nothing short of SPECTACULAR. They arrange a police escort like nothing anyone has ever seen. They turnout a pack of bikers 100 bikes deep and block traffic, putting their lives at risk— but no one will break through their lines to disrespect that funeral procession—NOBODY! They are professional and mission oriented. If there is an opportunity to have them at a funeral I highly recommend them.

Personal Note to the Patriot Guard:

I will be forever grateful for the Patriot Guard unit that worked our brother Shell Shock's funeral in South Georgia in the summer of 2016. They had scores of motorcycles there with huge American flags flying from the bikes. They called his funeral service a "mission" and were there to perform that mission. I initially argued with the commander because he wanted to lead the procession and no one was going to lead a Black Sabbath MC brother's funeral on a bike except a Black Sabbath MC Nation pack! The commander of the unit was not happy with me, but his superior quickly and professionally reminded him that he was there for us and immediately the commander relented. Out of respect I asked the commander to ride at the front of the pack next to me but his brotherhood rode behind our pack. I'm ever so glad that I did that because I was simply not prepared for the outright synchronicity and professionalism this "band-conductor" had planned the symphony of our brother's funeral procession—and he conducted his symphony like a true maestro! He had the police escorts arranged in every county as we brought our brother over 100 miles from Florida to bury him in Georgia. He had highway patrol, local police and sheriffs, who met us at every town and took us through to the next town where officers were standing at attention next to patrol cars in the utmost display of respect to our fallen brother. Officers would then jump in their cruisers, speed ahead, escort us through the town, only to again get out of their cars and stand at attention, hats in hands, as we got to the outer edge of their town to enter the next town. Then came the hand salute. Majestic! It was a site to behold. I wept with pride. Thank you Patriot Guard! Black Dragon BSFFBS.

The Last Rev

The Last Rev is a ceremony that many MC's use to send off their dead. There are variations to this ceremony but here are the basics:

- The Road Captain or the Sergeant-at-Arms signals the MC to gather as many bikes as possible as close to the grave site as possible
- The Road Captain or President gives the signal for the Last Rev Ceremony to begin
- All brothers will begin revving their bikes to make us much noise as mechanically possible
- The President or Road Captain will give the signal for all bikes to stop revving their engines

- The Road Captain will give the last, solitary rev of his engine

Grave Tending by the MC

Many MCs have yearly memorial rides where the brotherhood will ride to the grave sites of all deceased brothers in a particular city to pay respects at their graves. Often the deceased brother's favorite drink is spilled over his grave, from a bottle, and in some cases a blunt or a marijuana cigarette is buried near his grave stone (if he partook of such in life). When tending the grave of a deceased brother the Sergeant-at-Arms will lead the activities.

Grave Tending by Prospects

The Sergeant-at-Arms will assign the prospects to clean the graves and tend to them during the year, periodically, between memorial rides. Sometimes prospects may be ordered to ride hundreds or thousands of miles to tend to the grave sites of brothers, as a rite of passage for entry into the MC.

PART II SGT-AT-ARMS SOLDIER - SHERIFF

CHAPTER 10:
SECURITY AT THE CLUBHOUSE

The Sergeant-at-Arms is responsible for the physical security and safety of the clubhouse and every club member, visitor, civilian, guest, patron and visiting MC. The MC is legally and financially responsible for every person who sets foot on MC grounds. A wise Sergeant-at-Arms will PREVENT issues long before they ever begin.

Door Security & Bouncers at Functions & Parties

Where there is drinking, males, testosterone and machoism there will be the need for door security and bouncers. Most MCs use their own (in-house) muscle to accomplish this task. The Sergeant-at-Arms should not be lulled into thinking that just because a brother is a solid member of the MC that he has any idea of the responsibilities that accompany being a bouncer at a party. Because MCs are different than nightclubs, bouncing them is complicated and challenging. For instance, patrons (brothers of other MCs) seldom frequent a MC party alone. Normally they have backup and plenty of it. The wrong approach to bounce a member of another MC out of a clubhouse party can lead to a club war that could build up a body count quicker than one can imagine, so there must be training of the brothers and prospects to handle the complicated matters of motorcycle clubhouse security.

Best Bouncers

Many clubs believe that they need the biggest, toughest most intimidating looking individuals, martial artists or tough guys manning posts to present the most intimidating look they can muster. But the best bouncers don't actually bounce anyone. They simply utilize their good sense to display a presence throughout the

MC while keeping an eye out for unruly or overly intoxicated patrons, then act in a manner that will prevent trouble before actually allowing it to occur. Good security or bouncers manage people rather than react to situations.

Which Brothers to Use as Bouncers

Perhaps the better question is who NOT to use. Look for brothers with good temperament who have demonstrated maturity and sound judgement and are slow to anger. Avoid brothers with backgrounds in domestic abuse, assault or a history of other violence. Also avoid brothers with felonious backgrounds because if the MC ever gets sued for excessive force they can jeopardize the case.

Use of Force by Bouncers

The use of force to eject ANYONE out of the clubhouse should be avoided at all costs. Patrons can be hurt by getting thrown out into the streets and that can cause trouble for the MC. Remember that it is nearly impossible to spot a mental or medical condition by security personnel. Throwing someone in a guarded health down in the street could accidentally kill them putting the MC and the bouncer in a bad legal position.

There are common misconceptions that bouncers have the authority to pick someone up and violently throw them out of a clubhouse for a violation. Generally this is untrue. The most legally prudent way to remove someone from the premises is to ask them to leave. If that doesn't work call law enforcement and take out a trespass order. Typically bouncers can only use physical force when they are being attacked by a patron, as a means of self-defense. Even then only as much force as is necessary to stop the attack can be used. Excessive blows and punishment can land a brother in jail and lead to possible civil action against the club. The savvy Sergeant-at-Arms ensures his brothers know to keep level heads and their hands to themselves.

Physical Restraints used by Bouncers

Bouncers should avoid using restraints and compliance control holds to remove or subdue patrons. Headlocks and choke holds can be highly illegal and lethal. Hitting patrons in the head with heavy flashlights and night sticks can result in charges of attempted murder or murder, if the patron dies. Putting an obese patron on his stomach with his hands pulled behind his back, then piling on top of him could cause asphyxiation and kill him.

Controlling Anxiety in Bouncers

Studies have shown that cops in stressful situations often abuse citizens they take into custody after dangerous highway chases, fights, or shootouts. This is the result of stress and anxiety that clouds their minds and makes them think of revenge and punishment when they should be focusing on taking their prisoner to jail. The same can happen with bouncers. They can get so caught up in a situation where they stop thinking and start reacting. Thinking in terms of punishment and revenge rather than in terms of controlling the situation and quelling disaster. Young men enshrouded in machismo and bravado often want to compete and "dick-measure" rather than stay humble, professional and remain results oriented. Someone has to be thinking straight! The Sergeant-at-Arms must continually train his brothers and have safety briefings before each night's business. This ensures everyone's head stays in the game. He must also be observant so that he can order the brothers to a side room long enough to get everyone under control, to "re-start" them and get their minds once again focused.

Deadly Force Used by Bouncers

The United States Navy defines deadly force as:

Deadly Force is a **force** that a person uses causing or that a person knows or should know would create a substantial risk of causing death or serious bodily harm. **Deadly force** is justified only under conditions of extreme necessity as a last resort when all lesser **means** have failed or cannot be reasonably employed.

I wish that I could tell you that there would be no incidents where an MC would have to use deadly force in its clubhouse to protect its patrons or club brothers. I can only tell you that if it occurs in your clubhouse it most often is the cause of the clubhouse eventually closing down, no matter how just the reason. Also, because of decades old negative reputations MCs have, it will almost certainly result in one hell of a legal defense and lots of money spent by the club brother involved in the killing or injury. The focus should always be on mitigating issues before they get out of hand. Egos and machoism should be put down by the Sergeant-at-Arms and hot-heads disbanded before the ruin everyone's day.

Security Using Brothers to Handle Brothers

One of the best tactics for controlling an unruly member of another MC is to engage his brothers in helping to get him under control. Since most MCs do not tolerate outside MCs putting their hands on their brothers, the brothers should alert his Sergeant-at-Arms, President or senior brother that their member is causing a scene and their assistance is requested in getting him under control. This demonstrates respect and allows a potentially explosive situation to be handled delicately and professionally. The other MC will also be appreciative.

Inadequate number of Bouncers

Not having the right amount of brothers to act as bouncers can also put the MC at risk. The www.nightclub.com website states that "the hospitality industry minimum standard for guards to guests is 1:50 or 1:75; meaning 1 guard per every 50 or 75 guests." It is very important to remember that these industry standard minimum ratios are for the capacity of the venue only. So, in simple math, if the bar has a capacity of 200 people, using the minimum industry standard, one would want a minimum 3 or 4 guards, even if the guest count does not reach the 200 person capacity. For an MC, I would recommend doubling that number.

How to Break Up a Bar Fight

Of course I'm no expert, but in a March 16, 2009 interview with esquire.com, Geoff Gibbs, a nightclub security consultant, providing the following guidelines for stopping a fight before it starts:

> **Always** stay calm. Let your inflection and body language defuse the tension.
>
> **Never** make assumptions. You're dealing with intoxicated people who have nothing better to do than act like jackasses. So be ready for everything. Even vomit.
>
> **Step 1:** If two drinkers start arguing or shoving each other, stand directly between them. If you must, push them apart

but don't restrain. That only leads to calls to "hold me back," and that doesn't help anything.

Step 2: Identify the more aggressive patron and direct your attention to him. Shift his focus from the other would-be fighter to yourself, even if you're not quite as big as I am. Phrases like "Take it easy" and "It's not worth it" often do trick.

Step 3: Have someone remove the less aggressive patron while you're talking. Once he's out of sight, the fight will be over before it even started.

As well as providing the following guidelines for stopping a full-blown brawl:

Always get assistance. Not that you need an army — two sane people per fighter should suffice — but definitely have some friends keep the crowd back and watch for trouble. People rarely drink alone, and the lead jackass' pals might not like your interfering.

Never hit anyone. If you get slugged, don't retaliate. Your face and pride will heal. Your police record, not so much.

Step 1: If the fight is already on the ground, identify the more aggressive fighter (i.e. the one on top without his teeth missing).

Step 2: Standing behind said toothless fighter, put him in a half-nelson by sliding your right hand under his arm and up behind his head pushing forward.

Step 3: Pull his left arm behind his back. Use enough reasonable force to restrain him, but not so much that you break or dislocate a shoulder.

Step 4: Stand him up or force him to the ground, face down. Hold until he realizes he has no other options. Try not to use your knee or do anything that can leave a physical bruise. Because the good guy doesn't deserve to get sued, but he could.

Step 5: Once he's calmed down — or sobered up, though ideally both — let go of the main fighter but remain between him and his counterpart. Then make them leave the bar one at a time.

Step 6: Ask for a draft on the house and, because every hero deserves a prize, what time the bartender gets off her shift.

Bouncing Incident Involving Other MCs

If there is ever a situation where a brother of another MC is assaulted, or put out of the MC clubhouse, or MC event, the Sergeant-at-Arms should alert the President so that he can arrange an immediate sit-down.

To Search or Not to Search at the Door

That is the question! There was a time when MCs respected one another to the point that a person wearing colors would never bring a weapon into another MC's house. Those days are long gone. There was a time when Presidents were never searched at a door no matter what. Those days are gone as well. The Sergeant-at-Arms should always be more interested in the safety and best interest of the MC than he should be about decorum and appearances.

Hiring Outside Security

The Sergeant-at-Arms is responsible for examining each MC function and making the determination as to whether or not outside security will be necessary. If law enforcement or a security service will be used they will be under the direction of the Sergeant-at-Arms while on property. He will assign them and act is their liaison and manager on the scene. Ensure that outside security is not overly zealous when handling MCs and is at least familiar with certain MC protocols. For instance, make sure they know that Presidents get in free, or that Presidents are not to be handled in certain ways or maybe they aren't to be searched at all. The wrong interaction with a civilian security officer could get him broken up into little pieces at the MC's doorstep, especially when dealing with another MC's President.

Parking lot Security

The smart Sergeant-at-Arms controls the parking lots outside of his clubhouse or MC event. He does not allow loitering in the parking lot nor nefarious activities. He understands that bad things can happen in parking lots that are not properly policed. During the mid-1990s there was a killing the parking lots around the Black Sabbath MC every weekend. During that time kids from the neighborhoods hung out in the parking lots all weekend long. They wouldn't come into the clubhouse, they just hung out in the parking lots. Because gang violence was prolific in the neighborhood, violence would follow. It got so bad the city attorney decided to shut down the Black Sabbath MC and he nearly succeeded. (The full story can be found in the *MC Public Relations Officer's Bible*). Had we policed our parking lots properly, we could have avoided a lot of the problems we suffered back then.

MC Clubhouse Crime Scene

Unfortunately, a MC's clubhouse can become the scene of a crime if serious violence takes place there. The Sergeant-at-Arms should understand that mishandling a clubhouse crime scene will bring unwanted and sometimes dire consequences to the MC, up to getting the clubhouse shut down, or worse—incarceration of brothers for *Obstruction of Justice* charges and other sanctions. In the Black Sabbath MC's history, we have experienced murders and killings at or around more than one of our clubhouses. And even though no crimes were ever attributed to the Black Sabbath MC, each act of violence, committed by others, has been significant in diminishing the club's ability to continue operations at clubhouses where violence occurred. In one chapter, a murder from a shootout between rivals, that started in our parking lot and ended a mile down the road, caused us to eventually lose the clubhouse. In another case a man was killed inside one of our clubhouses and the homicide weapon disappeared as everyone fled the crime scene. Needless to say the police department's investigation of the MC was brutal, even though we had nothing to do with the crime, we were sucked into the middle of the investigation because we acted guilty, panicked and made unwise decisions. It wasn't until the actual perpetrators were finally tracked down that the police-hell was lifted off of the MC, but the by then the damage was done. The MC was never again the same and the MC eventually lost the clubhouse.

Unfortunately being a non-violent 99%er is not enough to keep idiots from bringing their baggage to your functions so if your MC's clubhouse becomes a crime scene the procedures are simple, especially if your MC is not involved in the crime. The bottom line is that you are not going to escape a police investigation with dead bodies littering the clubhouse floor, so take the smart and logical steps necessary to protect the MC. Think of a plan instead of simply reacting to a negative situation:

1. Preserve the crime scene for the investigation.
2. Don't let evidence disappear while the police are en-route.
3. Don't allow witnesses to run away, if you can help it.
4. Cooperation with the police may be the MC's only answer depending upon the circumstances.
5. At all times, operate in the best interests of the MC towards the MC's survival.

Remember, the MC didn't bring this crime to its doorsteps – someone else did. Let them be responsible for their own BS.

CHAPTER 11:
CLUB SECURITY AT THE CAMPSITE, FIELD MEET, FESTIVAL, ROUNDUP,

Campsite/Field Meet Site

In the old days the brothers would get together and ride to some destination like the Salton Sea in San Diego, California, pitch a few tents, and howl at the moon all night long. When lots of MCs got together we called it a field meet and everyone had a good time. Some field meets, like the National Roundup, Sturgis, and others are absolutely huge and can have thousands of clubs with potentially hundreds of thousands of bikers in attendance. Some MCs may pitch camp in a remote location just to enjoy peace, serenity and the company of the brothers. In either case, the security of the campsite is an absolute necessity. The Sergeant-at-Arms is responsible for the MC's camp setup and security, just like he is in charge of the setup and security of the clubhouse.

In the July/August issue of *Backwoods Home* magazine, in his article entitled *Small Camp Security,* Gary Lewis stated:

> "*It might be a sleeping bag in a lean-to with a small warming fire at the entrance. It could be a wall tent with five or six hunters high in the backcountry. It might be a recreational vehicle parked at the end of a road, a hiker's bivouac on the shore of an alpine lake, or a place to run to in the event of a natural disaster or unrest in the big city.*

> *Whatever the reason for the camp, chances are the camper or campers will have to leave, to hunt, to fish, to hike, to go for supplies. Camp is left unguarded, with no doors or locks — nothing between a thief and the potential loot.*
>
> *After dark, the camp and campers are also vulnerable to the creatures (four-legged and two-legged) that roam the night.*
>
> *Backcountry camps, both in and outside of established campgrounds, are vulnerable to theft and invasion. Camping equipment is hard to trace to its original owners and is easily converted to cash.*

No area of the country is immune. Homelessness and illegal drug use is rampant in the Northwest. Illegal aliens slip across the border all across the Southwest. All over North America, drug lords use backwoods camps for the manufacture of methamphetamines and marijuana grows. When we camp in the country, our nearest neighbors might be a family on their annual fishing trip, or felons on the run" (www.backwoodshome.com/small-camp-security).

The article went on to mention several other ideas for camp security. Below is my version:

Strengths, Weaknesses, Opportunities & Threats at the Campsite

The Sergeant-at-Arms should inspect the planned campsite for any strengths, weaknesses, opportunities and threats. If the worst should happen, is the site defendable? Does the site have cell service? If not, where is the closest cell tower to obtain service in an emergency? What are the access points to the site? And depending upon how long the MC will be at the camp, what effort must be put into re-stocking the camp with supplies and water?

Deterrence

Security works best as a deterrent when it doesn't have to be used, so it's best to setup the camp such that its appearance suggests security and causes would be thieves to look for softer targets. For instance, an unguarded camp is an open target for any opportunist, but if the Sergeant-at-Arms assigns prospects to a revolving guard duty around the camp site the camp will appear secure, causing even the most intrepid thieves to look elsewhere. Conversely, in a lax camp, where prospects are sleeping while on watch, grab-assing, or partying with the crew opportunities for exploitation will abound.

Keeping a camp site tidy and putting recreational vehicles, like four-wheelers and motorized skateboards in a central location inside the camp keeps thieves from walking past, grabbing that nice dirt bike from the edge of camp and making off with it. The Sergeant-at-Arms should instruct his brothers NOT to leave keys in their bikes and to lock all motorhomes and vehicles when leaving the camp.

A good camp design keeps tents close enough to be easily surveilled by the guards and good camp etiquette never leaves the site completely unattended.

Predators like bears, coyotes, wolves, etc. should be considered when setting up camp in a remote or wilderness location. Proper food storage is crucial to keeping unwanted beasts out of the camp. When camping with children in certain areas, children can also be vulnerable to predators.

Early Warning

In camps where a guard is not possible or the camp is located in a remote location – early warning systems may be necessary. Dogs are easy and time-tested early warning systems, but there are others. Electronic systems that establish a laser perimeter can be employed, but so can beer-cans on a string with coins in them hung at ankle level.

Night Light

Dark camps are great places for criminals and animals to lurk. Good camp lighting can alleviate dark places and make the camp easier to defend while offering a less inviting target.

Festival Site/ Roundup Site

Location, location, location is the name of the game when it comes to securing an excellent site at a festival. The Sergeant-at-Arms should know that it is most prudent to arrive early to get the better locations, because early arrivers get their choice in location when it comes to many biker festivals. At some field meets the traffic to get on and off the camp grounds can be tantalizing hours upon hours. Setting up as close as possible to the in or out gates could be crucial in efficiently getting supplies to the camp.

Shade

During the summer months when most MC festivals occur, nothing can be more soothing than some good, old-fashioned shade and a simple afternoon breeze. The Sergeant-at-Arms should scout for the best shade possible to help ease survival on hot, summer, festival days.

Flooding

Springtime festivals often bring daily showers that can make camp life miserable bringing flooding, mud, mosquitos, and humidity. The Sergeant-at-Arms should setup the camp on high ground and avoid low-lying areas where a sudden rain storm could cause flash flooding, or mud puddles that remain for the entirety of the festival.

Proximity

The Sergeant-at-Arms should consider how close the camp ground is to the main stage, bathrooms, trash dumps, and other positive or negative factors.

Condition of the Ground

The condition of the ground where the campsite is stationed should be an important consideration when selecting the location. Is the ground level, hilly or difficult to traverse? Is the ground rocky, smooth, covered with roots or tripping hazards, or level and inviting? Look for the ground to be as smooth and comfortable as possible, keeping in mind that pebbles, sharp rocks and other debris can puncture tents and be very uncomfortable to sit and sleep on.

Check the Festival Rules

The Sergeant-at-Arms should make sure that all of the brothers know the rules of the festival before they arrive on site. It would be very unfortunate to arrive at the gates with any contraband that is against the rules of the festival.

Control the MC's Space

In large festivals, groups will be looking to stick their tents anywhere. Once the MC has established an area, it must be secured and guarded until all of the brothers and their families arrive. The

Sergeant-at-Arms ensures that prospects rope off the campsite quickly because even a few minutes of inattention can give an unwanted squatter time to setup in an area of the chosen campsite that was intended for a brother. Since most festivals allot spaces on a "first come, first serve" basis, once a squatter has set up on the MC's campsite, it may become impossible to convince him to move.

Mark the MC's Territory
After the campsite has been established it should be marked with the MC's flags, banners and emblems. This will establish the MC's territory and make the camp easy to find amongst all the others.

Watch Out For First Day Thieves
Most thefts happen on the first day of a festival, while everyone is busy setting up tents and laying out equipment. Thieves can walk by and make off with valuable equipment, generators, motorized skateboards and the like.

Don't Bring What You Can't Afford to Lose
The Sergeant-at-Arms should remind brothers to leave at home what they cannot afford to lose and carry any valuables with them or locked in their hardened saddlebags. Motorcycles should be locked on chains to secure them. Bottom line – irreplaceable items need to be left home!

Stock Up
Supplies need to be stocked in large quantities as it can be difficult to get on and off the festival site to acquire more. It isn't uncommon for traffic lines to be an hour or more to get off the grounds and an hour or more to get back on them.

CHAPTER 12:
SECURING THE PRESIDENT

MC's Figurehead

The President is the figurehead of the MC. While on the Set and interacting with MCs, civilians, governmental and law enforcement entities, there can be no higher priority for the Sergeant-at-Arms than ensuring the physical security of his President. Simply put, if the President's safety is compromised the reputation and safety of the MC is compromised. Some folks might ask why a President of a 99%er MC even needs physical security. But the truth is, no matter how one's club is configured; law-abiding, criminal enterprise or something in between, all clubs operate on the same MC Set. Meaning there will be cross interactions and sometimes conflicts. A MC is expected to be able to hold its own no matter the situation. It must operate in such a manner that affords it respect and credibility, if it wants to survive. MC protocol calls for a MC President to always be protected while on the MC Set. He should seldom, if ever ride alone, nor should he be left unattended at events. He should be surrounded by prospects and then senior officers, like the Assistant Sergeant-at-Arms or the Sergeant-at-Arms himself and it is the responsibility of the Sergeant-at-Arms to manage any and all prospects who are providing physical security for the President.

Social Media and Presidential Protection

In the age of social media, Presidents today could face 'viral' criticism and scorn for controversial positions or stances taken on MC Set issues. In mere minutes or hours that 'viral' criticism can reach hundreds of thousands of people in cyberspace creating a serious risk from rival MCs and lone activists who are determined to make things right using threats, intimidation or violence. Social media adds another element of concern for the Sergeant-at-Arms who is trying to provide protection for a very vocal and outspoken President.

Executive Protection Program

The professional security industry has a term for providing security for executives, VIPs and presidents. It is called an "Executive Protection Program" (EP). To negate risks to MC Presidents and VIPs, the Sergeant-at-Arms should implement an EP to address each scenario where the MC would need to provide protection. The role of the EP is not just the physical safety of the President and VIPs, but also the protection of the reputation of the MC, President or VIPs. An EP assesses the impact to the organization should any individual be lost and examine threats, risks and vulnerabilities the individual faces.

Threats, risks, and vulnerabilities are separate concepts

1. A threat is a declaration or indication of imminent danger or harm.
   o Something will happen unless action is taken.
2. A risk is a possible injury or loss.
   o Something probably could happen.
3. Vulnerability is an injury or loss that is possible but not necessarily probable or improbable.
   o Something could happen although highly unlikely.

An EP evaluates each individual to determine if there are any active threats, examines their frequent travel to dangerous places, any criminal or dangerous situations to which they may be vulnerable, and the extent of their visibility. To establish a viable EP program for the MC's President and VIPs, the Sergeant-at-Arms must operate with a critical eye toward security. Educate the President on the importance of his security for the reputation of the MC. No situation should be taken for granted.

Initiating the Principle Profile of the EP

A "Principle Profile" is the set of security protocols to be followed when protecting the President, as established by the Sergeant-at-Arms. Depending upon the level of security the Sergeant-at-Arms feels is needed, as dictated by the current threat levels against his MC and/or President, the principle profile could be quite intrusive. The Sergeant-at-Arms should be afforded knowledge about everything in the President's public, private and Set life necessary to provide him effective protection. The President must give full cooperation when the Sergeant-at-Arms is constructing the principle profile during the EP.

No Bouncer Mentality

Many Sergeants-at-Arms believe that securing the President means surrounding him with the biggest, muscle-bound, bad-ass prospects the MC has to offer and then sending them on their merry way. But a mindless buffoon with muscles and a gun is the last thing a MC needs on the Set where MC wars could pop off at a moment's notice with little or no provocation needed to get things on and popping. True executive protection requires more brain than brawn. The Sergeant-at-Arms wants mature individuals who are not trying to prove themselves worthy of the MC by responding too heavy-handedly too quickly allowing a situation to get out of hand. The security team wants to prevent situations long before they occur by diffusing challenges before they erupt. The Sergeant-at-Arms ensures his security forces are specially trained to manage these operations with poise and class.

Make the Protection feel like a Perk

Many Presidents have a hard time figuring out why anyone would want to harm them until such time as they are being accosted by a rival. They often experience difficulty in accepting the watchful eyes of their security detail. It is the responsibility of the Sergeant-at-Arms to convince them that this any level of security is a perk of their office to which they are entitled and deserve. Educate your officers that their safety is imperative for maintaining the reputation of the MC.

A Healthy Knowledge of What's Going On

The Sergeant-at-Arms needs to have a healthy knowledge of the condition and general goings on within the Set. Information is critical in preventing crisis when executing an EP. The more the Sergeant-at-Arms knows, the safer the MC and the President. He should know which MCs are experiencing disputes or warring as well as any other threats or discord that may be loom. He must be an expert at networking with a penchant for spotting trouble long before it has a chance to develop into a problem.

Don't Forget the President's Wife and Family

If the President's wife and family accompany him, their safety and security should also be taken into consideration.

President Never Meets Alone

The Sergeant-at-Arms ensures that the President never meets another MC alone. The MC is a group activity it is never a team of one. There is no reason that a President should have to handle the MC's business alone in a meeting with another MC. A MC is at its best when at full strength and the President should only represent the MC's strength.

Case Study "Hard-headed President Wouldn't Listen"

For privacy, his name will remain a secret, but he was a friend of mine who was spreading his MC chapters across the country. He took it upon himself to get the blessing of another MC. Against the recommendations and instructions of the Sergeant-at-Arms, he decided he wouldn't need an escort. After all, he was an important National President. Long story short, the MC he visited was insulted that he would show up for a blessing without his brothers. They saw this as a sign of weakness, so he left the clubhouse without his colors. They were confiscated in trade for him getting out of the clubhouse unmolested. He never got a chapter running in that state. His cut hangs, upside down, in that clubhouse to this day. If he would have had his brothers with him perhaps he would not have encountered such embarrassment.

President is flanked on the Set

It is customary to provide a guard for the President on the Set. Depending upon the threat level discovered in the principle profile, the President could have one or several close escorts. They will assist, support and protect the President as he meets, greets and presses the business of the MC. His close escort usually consists of prospects under the guidance of the Sergeant-at-Arms or Assistant Sergeant-at-Arms.

Etiquette While Attending the President

When the Sergeant-at-Arms assigns a prospect or brother to guard the President there are some basic guidelines to follow:

1. Create a buffer around the President. Allow no one to get through without the President's permission. Be polite but firm.
2. Never interrupt two President's unless his safety is in jeopardy or there is some other urgent situation.
3. Never allow the President to put a cup down unguarded. If the President sits his cup down and turns his back, the close escort will pick it up, place a napkin over the opening and hold it until the President is ready to drink from it again.
4. Check the restroom before the President enters and, if appropriate, block the entrance and exit while he uses the facilities.

Prospects Security Services

The Sergeant-at-Arms will train the prospects to conduct security details for the MC, including:

1. Guarding/Escorting the President and MC VIPs
2. Guarding the MC's motorcycles at events and field meets
3. Guarding the MC's campsites
4. Standing as bouncers in the clubhouse (searching patrons, breaking up fights, ejecting unruly guests, etc.)
5. Guarding parking lots and conducting traffic at club events
6. Conducting funeral services and pall bearing for deceased brothers
7. Grave cleaning services for deceased brothers
8. Escorting the MC's women to their cars, from the clubhouse and from events
9. Guarding and escorting the MC's money drawer.

CHAPTER 13:
THE BIKER SET

The Set

The Biker Set or MC Set, commonly referred to as simply *"The Set"*, is where all bikers, who adhere to MC protocol and lifestyle, hangout, interact, ride and socialize. It is a mixture of places that combine to deliver the biker experience. The Set can be at a regular hotel having a "biker weekend"-- for that weekend that hotel becomes part of the Set, or it can be at a motorcycle club that is always on the Set. The Set can be at a park or a run like Sturgis or National Biker Roundup or the thousands of rallies, races, roundups, bike weeks, gypsy runs, bike shows and charity events that happen year round. Wherever there are bikers that adhere to the MC protocol and lifestyle hanging out and having fun, one will find the Set.

Who is on the Biker Set

Participants of the Set are 99%er MC nations, female MCs, riding clubs, motorsports clubs, independent bikers, biker chicks, groupies (male and females), hang-arounds, prospects, civilians, gawkers, wannabes, 1%er MC nations and others. These people are all somehow bound by the mystique of two wheels and are, to a greater or lesser extent, drawn to the lifestyle.

Sergeant-at-Arms Responsibility on the Set

The Sergeant-at-Arms knows that his MC's reputation, ranking and status can be easily effected by how it conducts itself while operating and handling its business on the Set. He knows that one incident, handled the wrong way, could irreparably damage the reputation of the MC forever. His responsibilities are:

- Prevent any discredit from falling upon the MC while it is operating on the Set.
- Ensure the physical safety of the President and club VIPs while the MC is operating on the Set.
- Ensure the physical protection of the full patch brothers, prospects, auxiliaries, support clubs, wives, blood family members and friends of the MC while it is operating on the set.

Sergeant-at-Arms Job on the Set

This list is not comprehensive, there are many more responsibilities I may have forgotten or have yet to encounter; however, this is a good primer:

- Ensure the Road Captain's "Kick Stands Up" time is adhered to by the MC, when leaving for events
- Set the MCs posture while at a particular event
  - Among family
  - Among friends
  - Relaxed
  - On guard
  - War-like
  - DEFCON 5
  - Attack
- Ensure the President has the appropriate number of prospects and security escorting him

- Ensure that an emergency escape plan has been communicated to the brothers
- Ensure there is a muster location in case the MC must bugout of the event quick, fast, and in a hurry
- Ensure communication systems are operational
- Ensure there are lookouts posted in case adversary MCs are expected to arrive
- Ensure uniform standards for vests and cuts are enforced
- Ensure Captain, Road Captain and Sergeant-at-Arms have synchronized their chronometers
- Ensure that the MC is looking good

On the Set, the Sergeant-at-Arms constantly monitors the conduct of the brothers, the location and security of the President, the temperament of the environment and he scans for potential threats. His main concern is to prevent hazards before they occur. He will use his Assistant Sergeant-at-Arms or deputize brothers as need be. If his MC is generally peaceful and gets along well with everyone, his job is easier. If not, then he should work with his brothers to resolve conflicts and find peace so that his job can get easier. He allows the President, Vice President and other officers to politic and mingle, his main concern is the safety of the herd. He's working hard while others may be inattentive. He sees if a brother is having a little too much to drink he instructs the brothers and the prospects to usher him from harm's way—or to escort him home. He watches everything. He never sleeps!

CHAPTER 14:
WAGING WAR

The ugly truth is even 99%er MCs may find that they have to wage war to protect themselves. Peace is a luxury that sometimes has to be fought for in order to attain. No matter how much one tries to avoid trouble sometimes it is unavoidable and the only options are: fight, die, or surrender and live as less-than-men. The aspects of any MC going to war, however, are bleak and seldom are the benefits worth the sacrifices.

Most MCs simply don't have the resources to wage war. Imagine what it takes to take an army to the battleground. The war command must be able to transport the army to the field, manage the support effort (including pay, dispersing, medical, dental, and vacations of its warriors), provide weaponry, ammunition (including supply lines and fuel), training and logistics Therefore, it is plain to see that a MC would have to be very wealthy to wage the kind of war necessary to completely eliminate an opposing MC. So, for the most part MCs don't truly wage all-out war, instead they partake in skirmishes. These skirmishes can last for years and leave broken and dead bodies scattered across the region all while accomplishing absolutely nothing. Since it is difficult for one MC to completely eliminate another, they effectively skirmish back and forth, sometimes for many decades—some fighting their forefather's wars, not even knowing why they are fighting in the first place. No matter how impractical a war may seem, sometimes MCs have to go to battle.

If waging war has been decided upon by the votes of full-patched brothers and upon the orders of the executive committee, the

Sergeant-at-Arms will have no choice than to advise his MC on how to wage war and, more importantly, how to win the conflict.

In his August 14, 2014 article for www.businessinsider.com entitled *"33 War Strategies that Will Help You Win in Business", Richard Feloni* summarized renowned author Robert Greene's *"The 33 Strategies of War"*. I have adapted and summarized both men as a guideline for the Sergeant-at-Arms leading a warring MC:

MC Warfare

1. Declare war on your enemies
Recognizing the enemy is paramount to defeating it. Do not be in denial. When an enemy shows, through its actions, that it is a danger to the survival of the MC, declare war on the enemy. Allow its existence to fill the brothers with passion and direction toward winning at all costs.

2. Do not fight the last war
The last war was yesterday's news. Today's war is where the focus is. Do not be lulled into complacency because of the victories of yesterday. Give each enemy the correct value and the respect it deserves. Underestimating the opponent can be deadly.

3. Amidst the turmoil of events, do not lose presence of mind.
In the heat of battle the Sergeant-at-Arms must be able to think straight. He must remain strategic to effectively command the MC in battle. He will not allow fear and chaos and the distraction of the battlefield to weaken his mind. He will concentrate and focus on the tasks at hand.

4. Create a sense of urgency.

If it is time for war then urgency is paramount. If the MC has voted for it then it will take place, or if the MC is forced to defend its clubhouse or territory, then the Sergeant-at-Arms cannot be caught in the delusion of hoping for things as they should be rather than how they are. Procrastination is worse than any enemy the MC may face. The Sergeant-at-Arms must create a sense of urgency among his brothers so that the MC is not caught flat-footed and off guard. During war, the sentinels must always be in place so that the army is never caught sleeping.

Organized Warfare

5. Avoid the snares of groupthink.

To lead men into battle the Sergeant-at-Arms must have their trust and respect. Without it, the brothers will doubt him and second guess his orders. On the battlefield the commander's word must be law. His vision is the strategy and his path is the way, if not, the war will be lost before it has even begun. The Sergeant-at-Arms must be able to think independently and reason for himself. He must be able to see the feint and misdirection clearly. He must not fall for the trap! Something that appears straight forward and easy to figure, probably is not. The Sergeant-at-Arms must be suspicious of the obvious and demand proof of everything. He must remember that nothing is as simple as it seems. Every tongue has an agenda attached. He must not be spurned into action with half-truths and uninvestigated facts. Even his own brothers must be observed with a critical eye.

6. Segment the forces.

When lacking the strength in numbers of a conventional army or when battling an army of vastly greater forces, guerilla warfare should be employed. The Sergeant-at-Arms must segment his forces into autonomous commando units, ensuring each is capable of holding its own. Then hit and run, plaguing the enemy with death and destruction before disappearing before their eyes leaving them nothing to fight. Terrorize them in their hearts, minds and souls, breaking their will to fight.

7. Transform the war into a crusade.

The Sergeant-at-Arms must inspire his brothers to become super-human fighting machines. He not only gives them a reason to fight for the MC, he gives them permission to die for the MC. He must transform the minds of men into a cause of "We" and remove from their thinking the sacrifice of "Me." He must build in them a hatred of the enemy so mighty that they understand that the greater success of the MC winning is worth every personal sacrifice and individual loss.

Defensive Warfare

A defensive strategy must be good if it is to withstand a sustained attack. A Sergeant-at-Arms should never be cocky or arrogant because they are traits for underestimating the enemy. Even Goliath was attacked successfully by David because he had fell victim to underestimating the enemy and consequently had no defensive strategy when that enemy attacked. The Sergeant-at-Arms should instead ensure his defense is solid.

8. Pick the MC's battles carefully.

It is said by veterans the world over that "War is hell." Consequently, the Sergeant-at-Arms realizes that whenever the MC engages in war there will always be hell to pay. There are residual and hidden costs associated with a war that can tax the MC long after the battle has been fought. Police investigations, funerals, reprisals, negative media and court battles costing tens of thousands or even hundreds of thousands of dollars. Often, a MC fails to survive even if it won the war. Effort should be given to seek other ways to resolve conflict and avoid battle. Remember, warriors never go to battle over pride.

9. Turn the tables.

The Sergeant-at-Arms will not be so brash as to believe that he must always have to strike first. The counter-strike is often the most decisive blow, because it requires cunning and patience to lull an enemy into an overly confident first-strike—leaving his flanks exposed for your counter-strike, timed to hit at the most devastating instant.

10. Create a threatening presence.

The best battle-win an MC can experience is the battle won, but never fought. If the MC's presence is threatening enough even superior enemies will steer clear for fear that the cost of winning will be too great.

In an article written by Forest Parks (March 14, 2016) for UrbanIntellectuals.com, entitled *"The Empress Candace of Ethiopia, 332 BC, Who Humiliated Alexander The Greek!"*, he tells the story of a threatening presence when an Ethiopian general named Empress Candace of Meroe, also known as Amanirenas, squared off against the historic general Alexander the Great on the field of battle. The article gives two accounts about the story:

> *"The wildly accepted first view, given by Chancellor Williams, who wrote "The Destruction of Black Civilization" is that upon hearing Alexander the great coming Empress Candace gathered her black troops, lined them up across the first cataract along with herself and stood on top of two African Elephants on a throne and waited for Alexander to show up. Alexander the "great", didn't want to chance a loss and give up his undefeated winning streak. He definitely didn't want to lose it to a woman so once seeing the black Queen on her Elephants and her black armies along with her, Alexander the "great" halted his armies at the first cataract, and turned back up into Egypt. Once he saw the deadly military tactician in all her glory and her black army with the latest iron weapons, he decided against an invasion and turned around.*
>
> *The other view offered by William Leo Hansberry says that Alexander met semi-privately with Candace. Legend has it that Candace advised Alexander to leave the region immediately and if he refused, after defeating his army, she would cut off his head and roll it down a hill. You use your imagination and pick which one happened!"* (http://urbanintellectuals.com/2016/03/14/empress-candace-ethiopia-332-bc-humiliated-alexander-great/#ixzz4VIQVNL2W)

The threatening presence of a MC can win a war without ever having to fight a battle.

11. Trade space for time.

Sometimes the Sergeant-at-Arms must give up territory to gain time. Retreating is not disgraceful when a stronger enemy presses forward. It allows the MC time to rebuild while its officers devise a new stratagem. There is a power in the strategic refusal to stand and fight.

During the Patriotic War of 1812, Napoleon lead his Grande Armee of over 600,000 soldiers into Russia on June 24, 1812. His aim was to engage the Russians in war to compel Tsar Alexander I of Russia into war. The Russians, however would not fight. They retreated deeper and deeper into Russian territory, burning their own crops, villages and towns as they went, denying the French any local food or supplies, forcing them to attempt to maintain impossibly long supply lines they could not defend. The Russians retreated all the way to Moscow and still, after a large battle there, they slipped away the next day, giving up the city. Napoleon made the mistake of pursuing too far and managed to get his men caught in the fierce Russian winter. His men were picked off, captured and executed as they tried to flee back to the border, while starving, freezing all while being ambushed by the Cossacks and local peasants. By the time Napoleon's Grand Armee crossed the Berezina River in November, only 27,000 fighting soldiers remained. Over 380,000 men died and over 100,000 were captured. In less than six months a mighty army was nearly completely slaughtered by a force that never truly met them in a conventional confrontation on the

battlefield.
(https://en.wikipedia.org/wiki/French_invasion_of_Russia)

Offensive Warfare

The Sergeant-at-Arms must not be pensive when it is time to carry forward the attack. The attack must be decisive and overwhelming. It must press and crush the enemy and is often best when it comes as a surprise.

Offensive Warfare

The Sergeant-at-Arms must not be pensive when it is time to carry forward the attack. The attack must be decisive and overwhelming. It must press and crush the enemy and is often best when it comes as a surprise.

12. Lose battles but win the war.

The Sergeant-at-Arms will not let the MC get caught up in small battles that have no relevance in winning the war. He will look beyond what is before him to a strategy that will shut down the enemy completely. If a small battle must be lost, as a means to win the war, he will not let pride or ego bog the MC down in an unimportant or irrelevant conflict.

13. Know your enemy.

The prudent Sergeant-at-Arms will learn the fighting habits of the commander of his enemy's forces. To know the habits, thoughts and maneuvers of the enemy's commander is to know the way the enemy will fight. The commander's troops are like an extension of his mind to fight as he has directed.

14. Overwhelm resistance with speed and suddenness.

The Sergeant-at-Arms will boldly strike the enemy and catch him on his heels, then strike again before he can regroup. Speed and relentlessness will frighten and confuse the enemy.

15. Control the dynamic.

The Sergeant-at-Arms will out-think his enemy by utilizing his forces to control the dynamics of the battlefield. He will play to his enemy's overconfidence by allowing him to think he is in control and leading the MC into a trap when actually the opposite is true.

16. Hit the enemy where it hurts.

The Sergeant-at-Arms will strike at the soul of the MC's enemy. He will find that which the enemy loves and treasures most and hit him there, damaging his psyche and even his will to live. This will destroy his enemy's will to fight by drowning him in his own personal sorrow.

17. Defeat the enemy in the details.

Even the most challenging enemy is not as impregnable as he may seem. Attack the parts that make up the whole and fight him on every level. He can be damaged politically, socially financially and physically. Spread rumors, sew dissension and attack his reputations. Cause hatred and fear among his club brothers by spreading lies and false accusations. Plant false evidence and frame him with spectacular tales of wrong doing in which he did not partake. Then sit back and watch the enemy turn on itself and destroy itself from the inside.

18. Expose and attack the enemy's soft flank.

Feint an attack on the front to draw him out and expose the enemy. After he has committed his forces towards the feint, strafe his weak flanks with the intended assault. The Sergeant-at-Arms realizes that attacking straight-up expends valuable resources quickly, while uniting and strengthening an enemy's resolve to fight back. For it is far easier to fight straight   than to battle the fear of the flank attack.

19. Envelope the enemy.

Envelope the enemy with unrelenting pressure tightening the vice until he can no longer breathe. Then continue to squeeze until he no longer have the will to fight.

20. Maneuver the enemy to weakness.

Endless revolving battles with an enemy is costly in lives, time and money. Instead the Sergeant-at-Arms should devise maneuvers for which there is no right way for the enemy to turn, thus ensuring that whichever way he moves he will be destroyed.

21. Negotiate while advancing.

Just because the enemy has moved into negotiations to end war doesn't mean that he has any intention of bringing the war to an end. Instead he could be using negotiations as a ploy to lull his opponent into a sense of ease while covering his attack.

Japan used such tactics to catch the United States off guard and strike without warning, as part of their plan to attack Pearl Harbor. Holding the U.S. into negotiations until just 30 minutes before the attack began.

(https://en.wikipedia.org/wiki/Event_leading_to_the_attack_on_Pearl_Harbor)

The Sergeant-at-Arms should continue to advance an attack, even while negotiating, thereby keeping the pressure on until the negotiations are over and the treaty entered. Such added pressure will cause the enemy to be incentivized to bring negotiations to a conclusion as soon as possible, so as to stop losing territory, while preventing him from launching an offensive during the negotiations.

22. Know how to end things.
Prolonged wars and battles put the reputation of the MC at risk and degrade the quality of MC club life. When it is time to end a war it should be done without any lingering skirmishes. The Sergeant-at-Arms must learn how to end things with finality, remembering that when victorious, he shouldn't humiliate or taunt his enemy, creating a bitter enemy that could strike back at the MC in the future.

Unconventional (Dirty) Warfare
War is dirty which is why it should not be fought in the first place. However, if a MC must fight, it must fight to win!

23. Weave a seamless blend of fact and fiction.
The Sergeant-at-Arms should not fear fighting a war with propaganda. To do so, he will need to create a false narrative the enemy will believe. By spreading rumors that the MC is not at fault even if it is, he targets winning the battle of minds and hearts.

24. Take the line of least expectation.
The Sergeant-at-Arms must not be so predictable that an enemy can correctly estimate his next movements. While making the enemy

think that he is predictable, the Sergeant-at-Arms' strategy should present the opposite. He should always seek to strike the enemy where be least expected.

25. Occupy the moral high ground.

The Sergeant-at-Arms will convince his enemy's political allies that his MC has the moral high ground—even if it is a lie. He will compel everyone to see how the MC has been wronged and that he is only protecting the MC from aggression. Make your enemy appear as evil and amoral as possible.

26. Deny the enemy targets.

The Sergeant-at-Arms will deny enemy targets at every turn. He will observe his flanks and keep the MC guarded. He will only move from a position of strength. He will not allow the brothers to fall into complacency. He will order them to maintain readiness, drill in marksmanship, and conduct themselves professionally. His goal is to never present an easy target, stationing watches when necessary, such that every attempted attack is costly to the enemy's bottom line.

27. Engage allies to give aid.

The Sergeant-at-Arms must compel the MC's allies to take up its slack where it is weak and unable to defend by establishing excellent family relationships during times of peace that can be called upon during times of war.

28. Give rivals enough rope to hang themselves.

The Sergeant-at-Arms manipulates schemers he suspects are working behind the MC's back. Feeding them false information and giving them the freedom to put that information in a place allowing it to come back full circle. Allowing the snitch/spy to be discovered.

29. Take small bites.
The Sergeant-at-Arms will target what the MC can handle without being overly ambitious or greedy. He understands that too meteoric a rise causes hatred and jealousy. He will keep his small MC in the shadows until it is too large for the shadows to contain it.

30. Penetrate their minds.
The Sergeant-at-Arms does not pontificate nor lord over rival MCs. He knows they will envy and hate the MC. Instead he will keep the MC humble and maneuver others towards the conclusions he desires, instead of their own.

31. Destroy from within.
The Sergeant-at-Arms uses his own spies to glean valuable information from the enemy. Allowing him to know everything that is happening within.

32. Dominate while seeming to submit.
The Sergeant-at-Arms makes an inferior position a place of dominance. By allowing the MC to appear submissive, when the opposite is true, he will win battles even against more dominant forces.

33. Sow uncertainty and panic through acts of terror.
Use acts of terrorism to spread panic, fear and indecision.

CHAPTER 15:
BUG OUT

Disastrous Events

Occasionally civil unrest, earthquakes, tornadoes, hurricanes, riots, revolts or outright war can cause a disastrous event to occur. During such times, if a brotherhood has determined that it will have an evacuation (bugout) plan to put into effect during a disastrous event, the Sergeant-at-Arms will develop and administer that program.

Bugout

A bugout is defined as:

> *Military Slang. A* hasty retreat from combat, especially in defiance of orders.

For any MC that believes in praying for the best while being prepared for the worst, a "bugout" plan is critical for being prepared for any event that may occur. An efficient "bugout" plan includes preparations for food, resources, first aid, clothing, protection (including weaponry and ammunition), and considerations for moving to a designated location, if necessary. The new location is typically setup in advance and is often referred to as the bugout location. Since it is often safer to bugout with a prepared group than alone, a disciplined, organized brotherhood is well suited for survival when the brothers bugout together. Below are my versions of planning for group bugout situations as interpreted from Sibi Totique's article for AmericanPreppersNetwork.com entitled *Bugging Out as a Group.*

Bugout Bag

The Bugout Bag (BOB) is perhaps the most essential tool in the bugout program. It can be one bag or several bags depending upon whether the bugout is on foot, in a bugout vehicle (BOV), conducted by an individual or a performed as a group. The BOB contains the implements necessary for survival while transitioning to a safe location. The BOB can also be referred to by several other names:

- Bugout Kit (BOK)
- Get Out Of Dodge (GOOD) bag
- 72 Hour Kit
- Grab Bag
- I'm Never Coming Home (INCH) bag

There are literally thousands of combinations of items that can be included in one's BOB. The critical thing to remember is that each brother (and possibly his family members and pets) should have kits that contain exactly what will be needed for the transition to the safe bugout location. When preparing a BOB, the following considerations should be made:

- Area of the country (travelling from and well as the area where you will be travelling to)
- Food/water necessary for length of trip
- Appropriate clothing for season
- First aid, prescriptions and medical needs
- Bugging out on foot or in a vehicle (each requires separate consideration)
- Implements of self defense

Note: *There are many books written on the subject of assembling bugout bags. There are even bugout bags for dogs and cats.*

Size of Bugout Group

In a situation that calls for an organized evacuation of a city or region, such as a hurricane, the MC could consider gather itself in one huge convoy, meeting in a centralized location and travelling as a unit to the safe location. In a situation more adverse that requires a more immediate response and/or requires departure on foot, the MC could break down into smaller groups while still travelling as a unit until everyone reaches the safe location.

Individual BOB and Group BOB

When bugging out as a group, a group camp setup will be necessary. Individuals will need to carry items required to setup the group camp as well as their individual BOBs. Individual BOBs will contain personal needs, while group BOBs should contain items needed for the group camp. The Sergeant-at-Arms is responsible for determining the list and distribution of items needed for the group camp as part of the Bugout plan.

When to Bugout

The Sergeant-at-Arms must ensure that the MC has established a basic set of conditions that will alert when the time has come to bugout. For instance, if authorities order the evacuation of a city due to a hurricane or other natural disaster, the MC's bugout program should be triggered. For a bugout plan to operate efficiently, the MC should have meeting spots as well as alternate meeting spots as a central point to gather and stage for departure. Backup communication protocols (such as walkie talkies or short wave radios) should be in place to allow the brothers to communicate should standard communication methods (such as cell towers) become unavailable.

Departure

After the MC has staged and is prepared to leave, a final meeting should be held to clarify all aspects of the bugout. Communications protocols, time synching, escape routes, alternate escape routes and planned rendezvous if any members should get separated from the main group, should be thoroughly explained.

Stops along the Way

When the evacuation plan requires migration over a long distances or over an extended period of time, such as across state lines to wait out a hurricane, overnight accommodations may be necessary. The Sergeant-at-Arms will set security details to ensure that the MC's vehicles and supplies are guarded while the bulk of the MC snoozes. During times of confusion the worst traits in people always surface. The safety in numbers for the group allows these members to sleep while dedicated brothers watch over them.

If the MC is making a camp for the night, the security precautions will differ, but the purpose will remain the same—protecting the MC's assets as well as insuring the safety of club members and their families.

Bug Out Vehicles (BOV)

Bugout vehicles allow the MC to cover vast distances, provide shelter and allow the transportation of heavy equipment and supplies but there are some drawbacks. BOVs require maintenance and fuel, which may be in short supply. During large scale evacuations, city roads can become gridlocked with traffic that can stretch for miles and cost valuable time for evacuees. It is not uncommon for vehicles to stall or run out of gas - blocking traffic from moving forward. The Sergeant-at-Arms should seek to avoid this confusion at all costs by moving the MC at the first window of opportunity or developing alternative escape routes using back roads and shortcuts. He must keep in mind that others familiar with the alternative routes may be using them as well contributing to the delay. . Other vehicles can be used to bugout such as:

- Motorcycles
- Trucks
- 4 wheelers
- Snowmobiles
- Boats
- Planes
- Helicopters

Stashing

Stashing is the practice of hiding stores, supplies, or equipment along intended evacuation routes. Stash locations can be brother's houses, storage facilities, or buried locations. Stashing allows the MC to replenish equipment and supplies while en route to the bugout location. It can also replenish supplies should the original supplies be stolen, lost or used The drawback of stashing is that one's supplies can be discovered and taken, or if the escape route changes the supplies will no longer be available on the new route. But it does give some peace of mind should the MC need it.

Example of items that can be considered for stashing:

- Weapons
- Ammunition
- Food rations
- First aid and prescription medicines
- Clothing
- Water containers
- Axes, Shovels, Hammers, Rope, fire starting equipment etc.
- Communication supplies and batteries

Equipment vs Skill and Experience

It is very easy to acquire all kinds of equipment to take on one's bugout journey. Selling prepper and survival gear has become a billion dollar a year industry. Every sort of fire-starter, direction finder, portable shower and more is available for those with enough money to purchase it. Still, no matter how many gadgets a group may have, they will not override the importance of the skill necessary to operate them. The time one needs to use a gadget to stay alive would not be the opportune time to try to experiment to learn how to use it. Practice makes perfect in all things!

Much more to Learn

There is a lot to learn and tons better resources than this book on the subject of bugging out. Every situation will be different and each MC's needs will be unique. This chapter simply provides some ideas about preparing your MC for the worst of situations during the best of times.

CHAPTER 16:
TURNOVER

Peaceful and Orderly Transition of Power

The peaceful and orderly transition of power is the hallmark of any democracy. The MC is no different. The Sergeant-at-Arms will ensure a successful transition of power to his successor once his term is completed. He will pass on as much knowledge as possible and all relevant information to his incoming brother. The transfer of power, documents, knowledge and information is known as a "watch turnover" in the United States Navy and it is a good term to use in this example. In the Navy one of the worst turnovers one could possibly give is called an *"I had it, you've got it"* turnover. In that scenario one watch-stander relieves another and the off-going watch-stander fails bring his relief up-to-speed with relevant information.

Physical Documentation

Physical documentation provides the new Sergeant-at-Arms an easy reference to draw a baseline from during his term. Documentation includes anything written that will be of value to the new Sergeant-at-Arms and includes:

- Notes
- Organizational charts
- By-laws
- Disciplinary files
- Executive protection program notes
- Rolodex information
- Email

- Correspondence
- Contact lists
- Procedural documents
- Meeting minutes

Turnover Meeting

During the turnover meeting the outgoing Sergeant-at-Arms will meet with the incoming Sergeant-at-Arms. He will describe the nuances of the job including his daily and weekly schedule and responsibilities. He will inform his replacement of any open and completed projects, challenges, situations and any advice he may have. He will provide keys, storage locations, and everything else necessary for the incoming Sergeant-at-Arms to successfully accomplish his responsibilities. He should attempt to give even more.

Glossary

1%er: Initially a description falsely attributed to the AMA to describe some of the MCs that attended Rolling Gypsy race meets. It was alleged that the AMA stated that 99% of the people at their events were God fearing and family oriented. The other 1% were hoodlums, thugs and outlaws. Non-AMA sanctioned MCs thus being seen as outlaws adopted the 1%er moniker and embraced it as an identity. Over time the 1%er designation became exclusively associated with OMGs, criminal biker syndicates and some OMCs. Though not all 1%ers are criminals it is certain that the 1% diamond designation attracts law enforcement scrutiny like no other symbol on a biker's cut.

5%er: A member of a MRO. Only five percent of motorcyclists are involved with MROs that are dedicated to protecting the rights of the other ninety-five percent of bikers by spending money, dedicating time and championing pro-biker legislation.

80/20 Rule: A requirement held by some MC councils requiring all blessed MCs within a council's region to demonstrate, via a bike count that 80% of the MC's members have operational motorcycles at all times.

AMA: American Motorcyclist Association

ABATE: An organization started by Easy Rider Magazine to fight against discrimination toward motorcyclists, mostly helmet laws originally. Once called "A Brotherhood Against Totalitarian Enactments" or "American Bikers Against Totalitarian Enactments", ABATE now has many other names including "American Brotherhood (or Bikers) Aimed Toward Education". ABATE fights for biker rights and champions many issues well beyond helmet laws. Members often help charities. Membership comes with yearly dues and officers are elected from the active membership.

Ape Hangers: Tall handlebars that place a biker's hands at or above her shoulder height

Backyard: Where you ride often—never defecate there.

Baffle: Sound deadening material inside a muffler that quiets the exhaust noises.

Bike Count: To stem the tide of the so called "popup clubs" some councils require a minimum number of motorcycles to be in a MC before they will allow it to start up in their region. MC numbers are proven when the MC undergoes a bike count of its members; usually with all members present on their bikes.

Black Ball List: A list enacted by a MC coalition or council. It is directed at non-compliant MCs that serve to notify other MCs not to support the "black-balled" chapter nor allow it to participate in any coalition authorized Set functions.

Blockhead: The V-twin engine Harley, 1984 - 2000

Boneyard: Salvage yard for used bikes and parts

Brain Bucket: Small, beanie-style helmet (usually not Department of Transportation (DOT) approved).

Broad: A female entertainer for the MC. She may be a dancer or at times a prostitute.

Broken Wings: A patch meaning the rider has been in a crash.

Burnout: Spinning the rear wheel while holding the front brake. (Conducting burnouts while visiting another MC's clubhouse is disrespectful as it brings complaints from the neighborhood and invites unwanted police attention. Make trouble in your own neighborhood and be respectful with noise and other commotion while visiting others.)

Cage: Any vehicle of four or more wheels specifically not a motorcycle.

Cager: Driver of a cage. (Usually cagers are thought of as dangerous to bikers because they do not pay attention to the road.)

Chopper: A bike with the front end raked or extended out.

Chromeitis: A disease associated with a biker that can't seem to buy enough aftermarket accessories (especially chrome).

Church: Clubhouse ("Having church" or "going to church" is referred to as the club meeting at the clubhouse).

CLAP: Chrome, Leather, Accessories, Performance

Clone: A motorcycle built to resemble and function like a Harley-Davidson motorcycle without actually being a Harley-Davidson motorcycle.

Club Name: Also known as a "Handle". A name given to a MC member by her sisters most often based upon her character, routine, quirks and/or a noteworthy event that happened in the MC of which that member played a part. This is usually a name of honor and often indicates the personality one might expect when encountering that member (i.e., 'Bad Ass'). This name is generally accepted with great pride by the member and is a handle she will adopt for a lifetime. For instance, I once became annoyed with a member of the Black Sabbath Atlanta chapter for giving me a hard time when I needed him to break into my house and get the keys to my trailer so he could rescue me from the side of the road in Little Rock, AR nine hours away. He gave me so much grief about my trailer registration, working condition of my signal lights and notifying authorities before he would break in my place that I frustratingly named him "By-the-Book" instantly changing his name from "Glock." By-the-Book so loved his new name that when he later departed the Mighty Black Sabbath M.C. Nation he took his name with him and is still called By-the-Book to this very day. (It is an honor for the MC to name you and quite improper for you to name yourself!)

Club Hopping: The frowned upon practice of switching memberships from one MC to another. Traditional MCs have low tolerance for bikers who "club hop" as this phenomenon breaks down good order and discipline in MCs. In fact this was seldom done in the early days. Most coalitions and councils regulate club hopping and enact vigorous laws against it. Often OMCs refuse to allow former members to wear another MC's colors after serving in their OMC. A MC should generally ensure that a club hopper waits at least six months before allowing them to Prospect for their MC unless the former President sanctions the move.

Colors: Unique Motorcycle Club Back patch or patches

Crash Bar: Engine guard that protects the engine if the bike crashes

CreditGlide: A RUB's Motorcycle

Crotch Rocket / Rice Burner: A sport bike **Counter Steering:** Turning the bike's handlebars in one direction and having it go in the opposite direction. All bikers should learn this maneuver for safety.

Custom: A custom-built motorcycle

Cut: Vest containing the MC colors. The name comes from the practice of cutting the sleeves off of blue denim jackets.

DILLIGAF: "Do I Look Like I Give A Fuck"

DOT: Department of Transportation

Drag Bars: Low, flat, straight handlebars

Evo /Evolution®: Evolution engine (V-Twin, 1984 – 2000)

Fathead: Twin-Cam engine (V-Twin, 1999 – Present)

Fender / Fender Fluff: A female passenger who is not an Old Lady but simply a lady a biker has invited for a ride.

Flathead: The Flathead engine (V-Twin, 1929 – 1972)

Flash Patch: Generic patch sold at meets and bike shops.

Flip: Occurs when an OMC takes over a less powerful OMC or 99%er. This can occur against that MC's will and could be violent. The less powerful MC will flip from their colors to the dominant MC's colors.

Flying Low: Speeding

Forward Controls: Front pegs, shifter and rear brake control moved forward (often to the highway pegs).

Freedom Fighter: A MRO member dedicated to preserving or gaining biker's rights and freedoms.

FTA: "Fuck Them All"

FTW: "Fuck the World" or "Forever Two Wheels"

Get-Back-Whip: A two to three foot leather braid with an easy release hard metal clip that can be attached to the front break handle or the clutch handle. Often it contains a lead weight at the bottom of the braid with tassels that just barely drag the ground when the bike is standing still. This ornamental decoration can quickly be released to make a formidable weapon to be used to slap against offending cages that invade a biker's road space (to include breaking out the cager's windows). Either end can be used in an offensive or defensive situation. The Get-Back-Whip is illegal in some states.

Hard Tail: A motorcycle frame with no rear suspension.

Hang Around: The designation of a person who has indicated that she formally wants to get to know a MC so she can begin prospecting for them.

HOG: Harley Owners Group

Independent: A biker who is not a member of a MC, but is normally a well-known, accepted individual of local Biker Set (of a higher order than a hang-around).

Ink: Tattoo

Ink-Slinger: Tattoo Artist

KTRSD: "Keep the Rubber Side Down" Riding safely and keeping both tires on the road instead of up in the air—as in having a wreck.

Knuck/Knucklehead: The Knucklehead engine (V-Twin 1936 – 1947)

LE/LEO: Law Enforcement Officer/Official

Lick and Stick: A temporary pillion back seat placed on the fender through the use of suction cups.

MC: Motorcycle Club

MM: Motorcycle Ministry (Also known as 5%ers)

Moonlight Mile: A short adventure with a lady friend away from camp.

MRO: Motorcycle Rights Organization. These organizations seek to protect the rights and freedoms of bikers (i.e., ABATE BOLT, Motorcycle Riders Foundation, American Motorcycle Association, MAG, etc.)

MSF: Motorcycle Safety Foundation

OEM: Original Equipment Manufacturer

Old / Ole Lady: Girlfriend or wife of a biker, definitely off limits!

OMC: Outlaw Motorcycle Club

OMG: Outlaw Motorcycle Gang

On Ground: Refers to showing up on or riding a motorcycle instead of showing up in or driving a cage.

On Two: Refers to showing up on or riding a motorcycle instead of showing up in or driving a cage.

Pan/Pan Head: The Pan Head engine (V-Twin, 1948 – 1965)

Patch: The back patch is the colors of a MC.

Patch-Over: Like club flipping a patch-over occurs when a MC changes patches from one MC to another. This is acceptable and not looked upon unfavorably in most cases. 99%er MCs patch-over MCs they acquire because 99%ers don't enforce territory. This will be peaceful gentlemen's agreement that happens unremarkably and without incident. 1%ers flip MCs.

Pillion Pad: Passenger Seat

Pipes: Exhaust System

PRO: Public Relations Officer

Probate/Probie/Probationary: A member serving a period of probation until she is voted into full patched (full membership) status.

Probation: The period of time a Probie must serve before full membership is bestowed. This is the time distinguished from being a hang-around because the member is voted into the Probie status and is permitted to wear some form of the MCs colors. The Probie is also responsible to follow the MC's bylaws.

Prospect: A member serving a prospectship until she is voted into full patched (full membership) status.

Prospectship: The period of time a Prospect must serve before a vote for full membership is held. This is the time distinguished from being a hang-around because the prospective member is voted into the Prospect status and permitted to wear some form of the MCs colors. The Prospect is also responsible to follow the MC's bylaws.

Rags: Club colors or a Cut.

Rat Bike: A bike that has not been maintained or loved.

RC: Riding Club. A group that rides for enjoyment (perhaps under a patch) but members do not incur the responsibility of sisterhood to the level of a traditional MCs, modern MCs or OMCs. Members generally purchase their patches and don't often Prospect/Probie to become members. Rides and runs are generally voluntarily and there is no mandatory participation. RCs are still required to follow MC protocol when operating on the MC Set and would do well to know the MC laws and respect them so as not to wind up in any kinds of altercations.

Revolution™: The Revolution engine, Harley-Davidson's first water-cooled engine (V-Twin, 2002 – Present)

RICO Act: Racketeer Influenced and Corrupt Organizations. Initially, these laws were passed for law enforcement to combat organized crime such as the mafia. They were quickly used to prosecute OMGs, OMCs and some 99%er MCs.

Riding Bitch: Riding as the passenger on the back of a bike.

Road Name: Also known as a Handle. A name given to a MC member by her sisters and is most often based upon her character, routine, quirks or a noteworthy event that happened in the MC of which that member played a part. This is usually a name of great honor and often indicates the personality one might expect when encountering that member (i.e. Bad Ass). This name is generally accepted with great pride by the member and is a handle she will adopt for a lifetime.

Rocker: Bottom part of MC colors which usually designates geographic location or territory, though other information may be contained there such as the word "Nomad".

RUB: Rich Urban Biker

Rubber: Tire

Rubber Side Down: Riding safely and keeping both tires on the road instead of up in the air—as in having a wreck.

Run: Road trip "on two" with your brothers.

Running 66: Though rare it is sometimes necessary to ride without the MC's colors showing (also known as "riding incognito").

Shovel/Shovel Head: The Shovel Head engine (V-Twin, 1966 – 1984)

Shower Head: The new Harley-Davidson V-Rod motorcycle motor.

Sissy Bar Passenger Backrest

Slab: Interstate

Sled: Motorcycle

Softail®: A motorcycle frame whose suspension is hidden, making it resemble a hard tail.

SMRO: State Motorcycle Rights Organization. Same as a MRO except defined by the state in which they operate, (i.e., ABATE of Oklahoma, MAG of Georgia, etc.)

Straight Pipes: An exhaust system with no Baffles

Tats: Tattoos

Tail Gunner: The last rider in the pack

The Motorcyclist Memorial Wall: A biker's memorial wall located in Hopedale Ohio where the names of fallen riders are engraved for a nominal fee (www.motorcyclistmemorial.com). Memorial bricks may also be purchased to lie at the beautiful site.

The Motorcycle Memorial Foundation: The foundation that operates the Motorcyclist Memorial Wall. P.O. Box 2573 Wintersville, Ohio 43953. **Thirteen ("13") Diamond Patch:** This is a patch commonly worn by some Outlaw MC Nations. The "13" symbol can have several meanings referencing the thirteenth letter of the alphabet, "M", standing for Marijuana, Methamphetamines, Motorcycle, or the original Mother Chapter of a MC. In Hispanic gang culture, "13" can represent "La Eme" (Mexican Mafia).

Three-Piece Patch: Generally thought of as being OMC colors consisting of a top rocker (name of MC), middle insignia (MC's symbol) and bottom rocker (name of state or territory MC claims). Not only OMCs wear three piece patches but new 99%er MCs should stay away from this design and stick to a one-piece patch.

Turn your back: A show of ultimate disrespect is to turn your back on someone.

Twisties: Section of road with a lot of increasing, distal, radial turns.

Vested Pedestrian: Is a person who is in a MC and wearing colors, but does not own a motorcycle. Often thought of as a person who

has never had a motorcycle, rather than someone who may be between bikes for a short period of time (i.e. a month or two).
Wannabe: Someone that tries to pretend to be a part of the biker lifestyle. (This is an excellent way to get your ass kicked!)
Wrench: Mechanic
XXF-FXX/XXFOREVER – FOREVERXX: Patch worn by MC members to represent their total commitment to the MC and every other member of that MC. XX stands for the name of the MC (i.e. Black Sabbath Forever Forever Black Sabbath).

APPENDIX A:
THE SERGEANT-AT-ARMS PROVERBS

Daily Affirmations to Keep You Strong

Do Not Take Sides in Club Arguments
I am the scales of justice in the MC. Yeah though there is a left view and a right view on every issue, the only view that truly matters is the MC's view. What is best for the MC is the only view from which I can see.

What Am I Doing Right Now To Better Serve the MC!?
In my daily MC-life practice I shall find myself continuously working towards achieving personal excellence in the service of my brotherhood. If the Sergeant-at-Arms is strong the MC will be strong!

I Shall Be the Example
If my brothers need an example by which to pattern themselves they need only look to me. I shall be the example of what a totally dedicated full patch brother should be. I will walk the MC, talk the MC, ride the MC, and live the MC. I am Sergeant-at-Arms, when my brothers see me they will see the MC.

No Brother Outride the Sergeant-at-Arms
My bike will be an expansion of myself. When the Sergeant-at-Arms rides they will know why I am a leader within my nation! I am a pounder!

I Am the Oracle of this MC's History

I am the keeper of tradition, customs, regalia, history and knowledge of how this MC was forged. Who will know more than the Sergeant-at-Arms about what it is that I am charged to manage?

Always Fair

All will be treated fairly under my watch. If fairness cannot come from me, who then shall bring it?

Due Process is the Rule of the MC!

There will be no political agendas on my watch. The bylaws guarantee our brothers certain rights. I will not let popularity nor lack thereof keep any brother from receiving the due process is he promised by our bylaws.

MC Set Awareness

I will have my finger on the pulse of the MC Set. I will know where the areas are safe for my brothers tread and when we should travel prepared for calamity or war.

I shall be an Ambassador of My MC

The wise Prospect will tell herself, "It is my greatest hope that I bring nothing but honor and praises upon my MC. I shall conduct myself in my dealings upon the Biker Set, at all times, as an ambassador of my MC."

I Shall Surrender My Ego

The wise Prospect will tell herself, "I am determined to serve my MC with all that I am worth. My full patched sisters depend upon me. To my MC I will give my utmost!"

APPENDIX B:
SERGEANT-AT-ARMS READINESS TEST

This test is by no means all-inclusive but you can use it as a guide to test the information you've learned in this book:

1. What are the author's four definitions of the Sergeant-at-Arms?
2. What are the two main definitions of Serjeants?
3. What are the origins of the Military Sergeant-at-Arms?
4. What were personal attendants assigned to the Monarch called?
5. Why do the Serjeants-at-Arms constitue the oldest royal bodyguard in England?
6. Who was Kevin Vickers?
7. Who was Corporal Natan Cirillo?
8. In what year did the British House of Commons receive its first Serjeant-at-Arms?
9. In what year did the First Congress receive its first Sergeant-at-Arms?
10. What are the minimum qualifications of the Sergeant-at-Arms?
11. What are bylaws?
12. What position is the Sergeant-at-Arms in the chain of command?
13. What does "Best for the MC" mean to the Sergeant-at-Arms?
14. What is the Sergeant-at-Arms' stance towards an active threat to the position of the Presidency?

15. Why should the Sergeant-at-Arms support the President in a coup?

16. Should the Sergeant-at-Arms support the President over the bylaws?

17. How is the Sergeant-at-Arms the liaison between the executive board and the members of the MC?

18. What is the chain of command of your MC?

19. What is the job of the President?

20. What is the job of the Vice President?

21. What is the job of the Secretary?

22. What is the job of the Treasurer?

23. What is the job of the Road Captain?

24. What is the definition of a lifer?

25. What is the definition of an active Full Patch brother?

26. What is the job of a Prospect?

27. What is an ex-member?

28. What is a friend of the MC?

29. What is an associate of the MC?

30. When the brothers are under the guidance of a good leader, where does it show?

31. What is leadership in an MC?

32. What are a sponsor's responsibilities?

33. What are 12 duties accepted from the Sergeant-at-Arms?

34. What is meant by the phrase "Courteous and consistent treatment", as it relates to the Sergeant-at-Arms position?

35. What is meant by the phrase, "Fair play" as it relates to the Sergeant-at-Arms position?

36. Describe the theory of "Politics vs Fair play as it relates to the Sergeant-at-Arms position.

37. What are five keys to being sought after as a senior officer to which club members can confide?

38. What are the two basic steps to handling grievances?
39. What are club meetings called?
40. Why are cell phones or recording devices not allowed in church?
41. How should the Sergeant-at-Arms deal with weapons in church?
42. What kinds of issues are resolved in church?
43. What are the Sergeant-at-Arms responsibilities before church service?
44. What are the Sergeant-at-Arms responsibilities after church?
45. What is Parliamentary Procedure?
46. What is ensured at the heart of Parliamentary Procedure?
47. What country did Parliamentary Procedure come from?
48. What are the four basic tenants of conducting productive meetings?
49. What is procedural authority?
50. What are Robert's Rules of Order?
51. What is the Parliamentary Procedure order of business?
52. What is the Parliamentary Procedure definition of a meeting?
53. What is the Parliamentary Procedure definition of a quorum?
54. What is the Parliamentary Procedure definition of speaking?
55. What is the Parliamentary Procedure definition of voting?
56. What is the Parliamentary Procedure definition of a majority?

57.   What is the Parliamentary Procedure definition of a majority?

58.   What is the Parliamentary Procedure definition of two-thirds?

59.   What is the Parliamentary Procedure definition of unanimous?

60.   What is the Parliamentary Procedure definition of breaking ties?

61.   What is the Parliamentary Procedure definition of main motions?

62.   What is the Parliamentary Procedure definition of secondary motions?

63.   What is the Parliamentary Procedure definition of suspension of the rules?

64.   What is the Parliamentary Procedure definition of an appeal?

65.   What is the Parliamentary Procedure definition of recess?

66.   What is the Parliamentary Procedure definition of fixing the time to adjourn?

67.   What is the Parliamentary Procedure definition of adjourning?

68.   What is the purpose of a judicial or disciplinarian board?

69.   What are some reasons that a brother may have a judicial or disciplinarian board convened against him?

70.   What is due process?

71.   What are the elements of due process?

72.   What is the composition of a judicial or disciplinarian board?

73.   How is the judicial or disciplinarian board hearing conducted?

74.   What is a suspension proceeding?

75. When is a suspension hearing held?
76. What are expulsion proceedings?
77. What is a negotiation?
78. Why negotiate?
79. What are the stages of negotiation?
80. What is mediation?
81. What are the stages of mediation?
82. What is the purpose of goal setting?
83. What is a goal?
84. What is a milestone?
85. Why is the Sergeant-at-Arms in charge of the clubhouse budget?
86. Why is communicating so important to the Sergeant-at-Arms?
87. What training does the Sergeant-at-Arms conduct?
88. What is the Sergeant-at-Arms' responsibility for safety in the clubhouse?
89. What is the Sergeant-at-Arms' responsibility for working conditions in the clubhouse?
90. What is the responsibility of the Sergeant-at-Arms' for working conditions at the clubhouse?
91. What is the Sergeant-at-Arms' responsibility for women involved with the MC?
92. What is the Sergeant-at-Arms' responsibility for sexual harassment policies in the clubhouse for external workers?
93. What are the two types of sexual harassment?
94. What is a sexual harassment policy?
95. What is a discrimination policy?
96. How should the Sergeant-at-Arms evaluate brothers?
97. What is the Sergeant-at-Arms' responsibility for data processing and social media and the MC?

98. What is the Sergeant-at-Arms' responsibility for maintaining traditions, regalia, and rituals?

99. How does the Sergeant-at-Arms' responsibility for writing a budget?

100. What is a duty roster?

101. What is a check-in log?

102. What is a field day?

103. Why should the Sergeant-at-Arms be concerned with neighboring structures and parking lots after club events?

104. What are the Sergeant-at-Arms' responsibilities for bar stocking and bar equipment and cleanliness?

105. What are the Sergeant-at-Arms' responsibilities for kitchen cleanliness in the clubhouse?

106. Why does the Sergeant-at-Arms interact with prospect sponsors?

107. Why is the Sergeant-at-Arms responsible for the club's hazing of prospects?

108. What are the responsibilities of the Sergeant-at-Arms during an event of injury, death or funeral of a club member?

109. What is the purpose of a media blackout during a crisis?

110. Who should perform next of kin notifications in the club?

111. What is the Sergeant-at-Arms' responsibility for supporting members and their families at the hospital?

112. What are the Sergeant-at-Arms' responsibilities at funerals?

113. Whose security is the Sergeant-at-Arms responsible for in the clubhouse?

114. What are the best traits found in good bouncers?

115. What are some consideration bouncers should consider when using force?
116. What are some considerations that should be employed while using physical restraints?
117. What is the definition of deadly force?
118. What are the safety steps to consider when breaking up a bar room fight?
119. What are the Sergeant-at-Arms' responsibilities when considering whether or not to search at the door?
120. When should the Sergeant-at-Arms hire outside security?
121. Why should the Sergeant-at-Arms control the parking lot?
122. What are some considerations for the Sergeant-at-Arms if the clubhouse should become a crime scene?
123. What does the Sergeant-at-Arms look for when determining the strengths, weaknesses and threats of the MC's campsites?
124. What does bugout mean?
125. What is a bugout bag?
126. What is a bugout location?
127. When should the MC bugout?
128. What is a bugout vehicle?
129. What does stashing mean?
130. What is an executive protection program?
131. What is the principle profile?
132. What is the proper etiquette while attending the security of the president?
133. What is the biker set?
134. Who is on the bier set?
135. What are the 33 steps of MC war?

APPENDIX C:
MIGHTY BLACK SABBATH MOTORCYCLE CLUB NATION BRIEF HISTORY

The **Mighty Black Sabbath Motorcycle Club Nation** is a national, traditional 99%er law abiding motorcycle club whose members ride all makes of street legal motorcycles (cruisers at least 750cc and sport bikes at least 600cc). The Mighty Black Sabbath Motorcycle Club Nation does not belong to any governing organizations like the AMA but is law abiding and is not a 1%er Outlaw MC Nation. It is not listed by the United States Department of Justice or any other law enforcement organizations as an OMC or an OMG. The Black Sabbath MC derived its name from the actions of the Original Seven African American male founders who rode on Sundays after church. When the Original Seven were looking for a name to call themselves—they said, "We are seven black men who ride on the Sabbath day after worship, so let's call ourselves Black Sabbath!"

History

The Original Seven founding fathers of the Black Sabbath Motorcycle Club Nation taught themselves to ride on one Honda 305 Scrambler in the hills of a neighborhood called Mount Hope in San Diego, California in 1972. That bike, given to 'Pep', by a close friend was shared between them. The founding fathers mostly worked at the San Diego Gas and Electric Company or were enlisted in the US Navy. They practiced evenings and weekends on the Honda 305 Scrambler until they eventually learned how to ride and each bought a motorcycle. Afterward they gathered at each other's garages after church on Sundays to ride, tell tall tales and drink beers. By 1974, their wives united and revolted demanding that no more club meetings be held in their garages on Sundays because the neighbors kept complaining and the wives felt threatened by the strength of the brotherhood. Undaunted the founding fathers rented an abandoned bar at 4280 Market Street where they remained one of the most dominant, influential and successful MCs on the African American Biker Set since 1974 (over forty years at the time of this writing). The brothers got their colors blessed by the Chosen Few MC Nation and the Hells Angels MC Nation in February 1974 after getting their clubhouse.

Founding Fathers

The seven original founding fathers were:

- **First Rider:** Robert D. Hubbard 'Sir Hub' (SDG&E Electrician)
- **VP:** William Charles Sanders 'Couchie'(SDG&E Electrician)
- **Sgt-at-Arms** Alvin Ray 'Stretch'

- **Road Capt:** Paul Perry 'Pep' (SDG&E Meter Reader)
- **Asst Road:** Capt: Solomon 'Sol'
- **Secretary:** John Kearny 'Black'
- Unnamed brother whose name has been lost to us

Racing roots

The Black Sabbath MC was not complicated in its mission during the early years. It was comprised simply of seven men who loved to ride, mostly on Sundays, who were similarly possessed with an insatiable appetite for custom building "Choppers" and unbeatable drag race bikes. This is still true today. All bike styles are welcomed and racers are most cherished in the Mighty Black Sabbath Motorcycle Club Nation.

Battle cry "I came to race"

The MC's battle cry was fathered by Black Sabbath MC legend, fabled racer, Allen 'Sugar Man' Brooks, who once wrecked Pep's motorcycle (early 1970's) at the Salton Sea bike run/race event, without a helmet, at over one hundred ten mph. Pep warned Sugar Man that his bike was not operating properly and was excessively vibrating when it got to one hundred mph. Sugar Man told Pep to let him test it and Pep warned him not to go over one hundred mph. Of course Sugar Man exceeded one hundred mph and destroyed Pep's bike. After the accident Sugar Man was forbidden to compete as the MC deemed that he was too injured to race. The President threatened to take his colors if he attempted to drag race the next day. Sugar Man said, "You can take these damned colors if you will. I came to race!" Sugar Man consequently won the drag racing competition despite his injuries thereby etching himself into the Black Sabbath MC's history books.

San Diego Mother Chapter

The Mighty Black Sabbath Motorcycle Club Nation's mother chapter clubhouse stood at 4280 Market Street on the corner for forty years. During most of that time the MC reined dominant as the most successful MC in San Diego and is the oldest surviving MC on the black Biker Set in San Diego. For decades the Black Sabbath MC clubhouse was the only clubhouse on the black Biker Set. During that time all San Diego and Los Angeles MCs came to San Diego to celebrate the Sabbath's yearly anniversary which was the first run of the year. Even to this day West Coast MCs gather in San Diego for the first run of the year established by the Black Sabbath MC.

Nationwide chapters

The Mighty Black Sabbath Motorcycle Club Nation has chapters across the United States from coast to coast but growth was initially slow as the MC never envisioned itself a national MC from its inception in San Diego in 1974. The Black Sabbath MC is the oldest surviving MC born in San Diego. The second charter was not given until 1989 some fifteen years after the MC started. Club racing legend Allen 'Sugar Man' Brooks took the colors to Wichita, Kansas where Knight Rider and Lady Magic, previously members of the Penguins MC, developed the chapter, subsequently becoming the oldest surviving MC on the black Biker Set in Wichita, KS.

In 1999, then National President, Pep, launched the Denver, Colorado chapter. Not long after, he assigned veteran member Leonard Mack to head up the Minneapolis, Minnesota chapter and two years later Dirty Red launched the St. Paul, Minnesota chapter. In 2004, Pep launched the Little Rock, Arkansas chapter with his nephew Lewis 'Doc' Perry who became the first East Coast Regional

President. Two years later Doc launched the Oklahoma City, Oklahoma chapter with his high school buddy James 'JB' Baker as President. In 2008, National Ambassador and former mother chapter President Dewey 'Jazz' Johnson launched the Phoenix, Arizona chapter. By then the Wichita, Kansas chapter was all but dead.

Exponential growth was not seen until 2009 when then National Enforcer John E. 'Black Dragon' Bunch II convinced Sugar Man to come out of retirement and launch the Tulsa, Oklahoma chapter. Black Dragon reopened the Wichita, Kansas chapter using hard core recruiting efforts but could not sustain the re-launch until Lady Magic tapped her son 'Pull-it' and grandson Chris 'Chill' Hill to restart Wichita. Black Dragon simultaneously launched the Atlanta, Georgia chapter with former Oklahoma City member, Pappy, who had also grown up with Doc Perry. Later in 2009 Black Dragon launched the Houston, Texas chapter with Bernard 'Krow'Augustus who became the first Midwest/Central USA Regional President.

In 2010 the Atlanta, Georgia chapter was taken over by Black Dragon's former submarine shipmate, Leon 'Eight Ball' Richardson who also became the first East Coast Regional President. Black Dragon became National President in 2010 and patched over the Macon, Georgia chapter under Curtis 'Ride or Die' Hill became the third East Coast Regional President. Black Dragon then patched-over the Sic Wit' It MC in Rome, Georgia under President G Man.

Sugar Man's first cousin Jamel 'Huggy Bear' Brooks launched the San Antonio, Texas chapter by the end of 2010 and became the first West Coast Regional President when he assumed command of the Phoenix, Arizona chapter in late 2010. Huggy Bear patched over the

Inland Empire, California chapter under the leadership of Big Dale in 2011. Big Dale eventually became the second West Coast Regional President. In 2012 National Vice President Tommy 'Hog Man' Lewis received a blessing from the Chosen Few MC to open the Las Vegas, Nevada chapter with then East Coast Regional President Huggy Bear. In 2012 the Jacksonville, Florida chapter was launched under President Prime. In 2014, West Coast Regional President Big Dale launched the Riverside, California chapter under President Bob O. At the time of this writing, there are seven more prospective Black Sabbath MC chapters seeking to gain entry. Hail to the forefathers of the Mighty Black Sabbath Motorcycle Club Nation! We hope they are proud of what their dreams have become. Amen.

Membership

A prospective member is allowed into the Black Sabbath Motorcycle Club as a "hang-around," indicating that the individual is invited to some MC events or to meet MC members at known gathering places. This period could last several months. It is the time for the hang-around to evaluate the MC as well as for the MC to evaluate the hang-around. If the hang-around is interested and the Black Sabbath Motorcycle Club likes the hang-around, he can request to be voted in as a Prospect. The hang-around must win a majority vote to be designated a Prospect. If he is successful he will be given a sponsor and his prospectship begins. The prospectship will be no less than ninety days but could last for years depending upon the attitude and resourcefulness of the Prospect. National President Black Dragon prospected for nearly five years before he was accepted. The Prospect will participate in some MC activities and serve the MC in whatever capacity the full patched brothers may deem appropriate. A Prospect will never be asked to commit any illegal act, any act against nature, or any physically humiliating or demeaning act. The Black Sabbath Motorcycle Club never hazes Prospects. A Prospect won't have voting privileges while he is evaluated for suitability as a full member but does pay MC dues. The last phase, and highest membership status, is "Full Membership" or "Full-Patch". The term "Full-Patch" refers to the complete one-piece patch. Prospects are allowed to wear only a small thirteen-inch patch with the letters of the local chapter (i.e. BSSD) and the black cross on it. To become a full patched brother the Prospect must be presented by his sponsor before the MC and win a 100% affirmative vote from the full patched brothers. Prior to votes being cast, a Prospect usually travels to every chapter in the sponsoring chapter's geographic region (state/province/territory) and introduces himself to every full patched brother. This process allows all regional chapter members to become familiar with the Prospect. Some form of formal induction follows, wherein the Prospect affirms his loyalty to the MC and its members. Often the Prospect's sponsor may require him to make a nomadic journey on his motorcycle before crossing over, sometimes as far as 1,000 miles that must be completed within twenty-four hours to ensure that the Prospect understands the Black Sabbath Motorcycle Club is a riding motorcycle club. The final logo patch is then awarded at his swearing in and initiation ceremony. The step of attaining full membership can be referred to as "being patched", "patching in" or "crossing over."

Command Structure

- National President
- National Vice President
- High Council President

- High Council
- National Business Manager
- National Ambassador
- Regional President
- President
- Vice President
- Sgt-at-Arms
- Road Captain
- Treasurer
- Secretary
- Business Manager
- Public Relations Officer
- Full Patch Member
- First Lady SOTC
- Full Patch SOTC
- Head Goddess
- Full Patch Goddess
- Support Crew
- Prospect
- SOTC Prospect
- Goddess Prospect
- Hang Around

Colors

The Black Sabbath Motorcycle Club patch is called the "Turtle Shell". The colors are set out on a white background inside a black circle, inside a black crested shield, with the words Black Sabbath MC encircling the riding man. The crested shield on the sixteen-inch back patch gives the appearance of a turtle's shell when worn as it covers most members' entire back. The MC's colors are white, yellow, black and blue.

In the forty-plus year history of the MC the colors have remained untouched except for the addition of the shield in 1975 and the enlargement of the patch to nineteen-inch by sixteen inch in 2009. The adherence to the original patch mirrors their adherence to the core values of the Original Seven founding forefathers.

Since the Black Sabbath Motorcycle Club does not claim territory like dominant 1%er MC Nations its members don't wear state bottom rockers. The cities of the chapters are named on the colors.

Racial Policies

Because the Black Sabbath Motorcycle Club was started by African Americans and its membership is primarily African American (90%) it is considered to be on the 'Black Biker Set" by biker clubs across America. However the Black Sabbath Motorcycle Club states that even though it was started by seven African American men who rode on Sundays, today it is a multi-racial organization that is accepting of all religions, with chapters across the United States from coast to coast. The Mighty Black Sabbath Motorcycle Club Nation is a brotherhood based on a unified lifestyle centered on riding motorcycles, living the biker lifestyle and embracing one another as extended family as close as any blood relatives.

Neutrality

The Mighty Black Sabbath Motorcycle Club Nation has followed all MC protocol in setting up its chapters nationwide. To that end it has received blessings to operate by dominants in every area in which it has chapters. As a neutral 99%er elite motorcycle enthusiast, riding MC the Mighty Black Sabbath Motorcycle Club Nation wears no support patches as it takes no political sides and does not align itself with OMC politics.

Women in the Black Sabbath MC Nation
Women fall into two unique categories— Women who ride motorcycles belong to the "Sisters of the Cross MC of the Mighty Black Sabbath Motorcycle Club Nation." Women who do not ride motorcycles belong to the female support auxiliary known as "Goddesses of the Mighty Black Sabbath Motorcycle Club Nation."

Sisters of the Cross
The Sisters of the Cross MC of the Mighty Black Sabbath Motorcycle Club Nation (SOTC) is a female motorcycle club that rides under the full patched brothers of the Black Sabbath Motorcycle Club. The SOTC was established in 2011 by National President, Black Dragon. SOTC Prospects must be eighteen years old, own a motorcycle and have a motorcycle driver's license. The SOTC are called the "First Ladies of the Black Sabbath Motorcycle Club" and the ranking SOTC is called First Lady. The SOTC MC was created to recognize the achievements of many of the Goddesses of the Black Sabbath Motorcycle Club who were buying, learning how to ride and getting licenses for motorcycles at an incredible rate. The Mighty Black Sabbath Motorcycle Club Nation sought to reward the hard work and passion to ride these women displayed by giving them their own MC under the auspices of the Mighty Black Sabbath Motorcycle Club Nation.

Goddesses of the Club
The Goddesses of the Mighty Black Sabbath Motorcycle Club Nation are the social club auxiliary that supports the MC. Goddess Prospects must be eighteen years old, be of exceptional character and devoted to serve the best interests of the Mighty Black Sabbath Motorcycle Club.

Mission Statement

" 1. To become the greatest riding motorcycle club in the world by pounding down great distances on two wheels, bonding on the highways and byways as family, camping out while riding to biker events or cross country, enjoying the wilderness, racing, competing, winning and experiencing our extended family by tenderly loving each other more and more each day!
2. To become the greatest motorcycle club family in the world by encouraging diversity within our MC, building strong, lasting friendships among members, instilling a sense of love, pride, and togetherness within our communities, by helping those in need through volunteerism, by cultivating a mindset of moral, social responsibility amongst our members. And by inspiring our youth to achieve beyond all limitations which will leave a legacy of hope and boundless dreams for future generations of the Mighty Black Sabbath Motorcycle Club Nation to come. "

National President

The office of the National President was created by Tommy 'Hog Man' Lewis then President of the mother chapter and former mother chapter President Dewey 'Jazz' Johnson, in the summer of 2000. Paul 'Pep' Perry, the last original founding member left in the chapter, was elected the first National President. Curtis 'Mad Mitch' Mitchell was appointed first National Vice President one year later. Pep also created the office of National Ambassador to which he assigned Jazz. The National Vice President position was eventually terminated. In 2010, Godfather Washington of the Mighty Black Sabbath Motorcycle Club Nation died and Pep retired to become

Godfather. National Enforcer and President of the Atlanta chapter, Black Dragon was summoned to the mother chapter in San Diego and was elected as the second National President of the Might Black Sabbath Motorcycle Club Nation during the February mother chapter annual dance. Black Dragon recreated the National Vice President office and recruited then retired former San Diego President Hog Man for the position. Black Dragon created the High Council President office to which he assigned Sabbath racing legend Sugar Man. He also created the High Council which consists of the President and Vice President of every chapter. Black Dragon also created the National Sgt-at-Arms, National Business Manager, Nomad, Disaster Chief, Support Chief and PRO offices.

Riding Awards and Designations

In order to challenge his MC members to ride harder and to distinguish the Mighty Black Sabbath Motorcycle Club Nation as a superior, elite motorcycle enthusiast riding MC, Black Dragon created the Nomad Rider program. In an article written in the Black Sabbath Magazine, Black Dragon stated, "A 99%er law abiding MC Nation is nothing if its members don't ride!" The Nomad Rider program recognizes and awards Black Sabbath Motorcycle Club nomad riders for their achievements. Some of the awards include:

- Nomad Rider = 1,000 miles one-way (N1)
- 1 K in 1 Day Nomad = 1,000 miles one-way ridden in twenty-four hours or less (N124)
- Nomad Traveler = 2,000 miles one-way (N2)
- Nomad Warrior = 3,000 miles one-way (N3)
- Nomad Adventurer = 4,000 miles one-way (N4)
- Nomad Wanderer = 5,000 miles one-way (N5)

- Snow Bear Disciple Nomad = one hundred miles traveled in sleet, snow or 18° F (SBN)
- Poseidon's Disciples Nomad = traveling through three states during continuous, driving rain (PSN)
- Great Plains Nomad = riding across the Oklahoma or Kansas great plains (GPN)
- Panhandle Nomad = riding across the great state of Texas (TPN)
- Great Winds Nomad = riding through fifty mph wind storm (GWN)
- 1,000 mile bull's horn = eleven inch bull's blowing horn, awarded to all Nomad Riders
- 2,000 mile Kudu's horn shofar = twenty three-inch Kudu antelope's blowing horn, awarded to all Nomad Travelers
- 3,000 mile Kudu's horn shofar = thirty three-inch Kudu or Blesbok antelope's blowing horn, awarded to all Nomad Warriors
- 4,000 mile horn shofar = forty-inch Kudu, Blesbok or Impala antelope's blowing horn, awarded to all Nomad Adventurers; can be Kudu, Blesbok or Impala.
- 5,000 mile horn shofar = fifty-inch antelope's blowing horn, awarded to all Nomad Wanderers; can be any horned cloven footed animal.

Violence

Violent incidents have occurred in and around nationwide clubhouses.

- In 2002, President 'Bull' of the Zodiacs MC was killed after he pulled a gun on his former Prospect who was partying at the mother chapter with a new MC in which he was interested. The former Prospect slashed Bull's throat with a knife when he looked away during the confrontation. This was the first killing ever committed at a Black Sabbath MC clubhouse and brought the city of San Diego down on top of the clubhouse. The City Attorney initiated a campaign to shut down the clubhouse, nearly finishing the Black Sabbath MC. The clubhouse was subsequently firebombed in retaliation for Bull's killing.

- In February 2010, the mother chapter at 4280 Market Street was again targeted by arsonists who attempted to burn it to the ground right before the 2010 annual. They were unsuccessful.
- In 2010, a man was fatally shot in a hail of gunfire outside the Phoenix chapter of the Black Sabbath MC clubhouse during an altercation over a woman. He died a block away while fleeing the scene. This incident caused the closing of the Phoenix chapter clubhouse.
- On 11 May 2012, San Diego mother chapter President 'Wild Dogg' was murdered in front of the Black Sabbath Motorcycle Club clubhouse at 4280 Market Street during a drive by assassination. The case is still unsolved and open.

Epilogue

"Everything that I stand so firmly against today, I once was! It is only through experience, pain, suffering and being blessed to learn life's lessons that I have evolved to whom I've become. "

John E. Bunch II

When I was coming along there were no books that one could find to give job descriptions and introduce ideas that might improve one's ability to perform their MC duties with more expertise and efficiency. Many of the things I have written come from experiences in failure, more so than with my experiences in success. Which means I can probably tell someone that they shouldn't do this, that way, because it failed when I tried to do it like that. In any event I will be most satisfied to know if any part of this book helps anyone. That was my only purpose in my pursuit to write it. No matter how you feel about it now that you have read it, I still say; thank you for taking the time to read my book!

Bibliography

[1] "Sergeant-at-Arms - The Speaker". speaker.ontla.on.ca. Retrieved 2016-02-03.

[2] "sergeant-at-arms: definition of sergeant-at-arms in Oxford English Dictionary". Oxford English Dictionary. Retrieved 2016-10-27.

[3]"Sergeant-at-Arms - The Speaker". speaker.ontla.on.ca. Retrieved 2016-02-03.

[4] "What Else Does the Sergeant-at-Arms Do?". Mental Floss. Retrieved 2016-02-03.

[5] "Serjeant-at-Arms". www.aph.gov.au. Parliament of Australia. Retrieved 2016-02-02.

[6] Robert, Henry M.; et al. (2011). *Robert's Rules of Order Newly Revised* (11th ed.). Philadelphia, PA: Da Capo Press. p. l. ISBN 978-0-306-82020-5

About the Author

John E. Bunch II 'Black Dragon' rode on the back of a Honda Trail 50 for the first time when he was six years old. Instantly he was hooked! His mother couldn't afford to buy him a motorcycle so he borrowed anyone's bike that would let him ride, on back roads and farms all over Oklahoma where he grew up. When he was 14 his mother bought him a Yamaha 125 Enduro. By the time he was seventeen his step father, J.W. Oliver, gave him a Honda CX500. He was known throughout the neighborhood as the kid who always rode wheelies with his sisters, Thea and Lori,

hanging off the back. He took his first road trip at seventeen riding from Oklahoma City to Wichita, Kansas to visit his Aunt Bernita and Uncle J.P. He knew then that he was born to distance ride! The nomadic call of the open road in the wind, rain, cold, heat—under the stars were home to him.

In the late 1980's, he found himself a young submarine sailor stationed in San Diego, California. He got into trouble on the base with a Senior Chief who gave him and his best friend an order they refused to follow. The white Senior Chief did not want to see the young black man's career ended over insubordination so he did Bunch an extreme favor and sent him and his friend, Keith Corley, to see black Senior Chief George G. Clark III instead of to a Courts Martial. Senior Chief Clark threatened Bunch and Corley with physical violence if they didn't obey the Senior Chief and worked out a solution that saved both of their careers. Later Clark invited them to 4280 Market Street when he discovered Bunch had a love of motorcycles. Bunch walked into the mother chapter of the Black Sabbath Motorcycle Club and was blown away to learn that the Senior Chief Clark was also known as 'Magic', former President of the Black Sabbath Motorcycle Club mother chapter. Bunch was consumed by the strength, unity and brotherhood he had never experienced before. He became a Prospect for the Black Sabbath Motorcycle Club. His insubordinate ways were not quite behind him, so it took Bunch several years to actually cross over as a full patched brother known as 'Black Dragon' in the Black Sabbath Motorcycle Club.

In 2000, Black Dragon began advising writer/filmmaker Reggie Rock Bythewood who co-wrote and directed the DreamWorks movie Biker Boyz. Black Dragon went to Hollywood and worked as a Technical Advisor on the film. Biker Boyz has often been credited with re-birthing the African American MC movement in the United States.

John E. Bunch II 'Black Dragon' BSFFBS

In 2009, Black Dragon brought the Black Sabbath Motorcycle Club to Atlanta, GA as President and an Original Seven founding member. He suffered his first setback in Atlanta during a coupe that cost him the Presidency of the Atlanta chapter in December 2010. In February 2010, he was elected to the office of National President and began his nationwide march to spread the Black Sabbath Motorcycle Club from coast to coast. By 2011, the Black Sabbath Motorcycle Club became the Mighty Black Sabbath Motorcycle Club Nation with chapters spread from the West coast to the East coast.

Black Dragon has published several biker magazines including: *Urban Biker Cycle News, Black Iron Motorcycle Magazine, Black Sabbath Motorcycle News Letter* and the popular blog www.BlackSabbathMagazine.com. In 2013, Black Dragon created the first MC phone app, *"Black Sabbath Motorcycle Club"*.

Today Black Dragon is building a Mighty MC Nation that rides cross country year round where no trailers are allowed! Black Dragon and Keith 'Alcatraz' Corley currently serve the Mighty Black Sabbath Motorcycle Club Nation as brothers of the Atlanta chapter.

Black Sabbath Forever Forever Black Sabbath
A Breed Apart
Since 1974

www.blacksabbathmc.com

www.blacksabbathmagazine.com

A Note from Black Dragon

Now what? You've read the book and you now know the power of the information held within. I want you to know that you can help other Sergeants-At-Arms navigate their way through the murky waters of serving the MC.

If you were helped, educated or informed by this book there are a couple of simple things you can do to join me in remaking the MC world through knowledge, experience, education and love – starting with the Sergeants:

1. Buy this book for a Sergeant-At-Arms or Assistant Sergeant-At-Arms in your MC. If you believe Sergeant-At-Arms Bible can deliver a qualified leader, servant and war chief to your MC then I ask that you spread the word by buying them a copy.

Give it as a gift or setup a reading group to discuss how Sergeant-At-Arms Bible applies to Sergeants-At-Arms in your MC. You can also write an honest review on social media, your blog, website, or on your favorite bookseller's website. There are countless ways you can help others by spreading this word. Sergeant-At-Arms Bible is not just a book worth reading, it's a vision and a plan worth following to improve the accountability system, security and adherence to the bylaws, in your MC. It is a vision worth sharing.

2. Enrich other motorcycle clubs by buying this book for your brother and sister MCs on your set or those with whom you share alliances. Imagine if other Sergeant-At-Arms could have the benefit of the knowledge you've attained.

Thank you for your support! Send me a note anytime with questions, improvements, or your best Sergeant-At-Arms tales. *JBll*

Other Books by Author John E. Bunch II:

Prospect's Bible "How to Join a Traditional 'Law Abiding' MC"

The Motorcycle Club PRO's Bible "Making the PRO Real"

Prospect's Bible for Women's Motorcycle Clubs

Kill Proof! "Surviving the Police Pull-Over, Renegade Cops and Vigilantes with Guns"

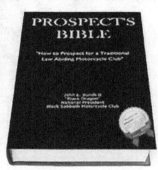

Books by Black Dragon on Amazon & Kindle

www.prospectsbible.com

Also available at www.prospectsbible.com

Kill Proof! "Surviving the Police Pull Over, Renegade Cops, Vigilantes and Angry White Men with Guns..." <u>www.thekillproofbook.com</u>

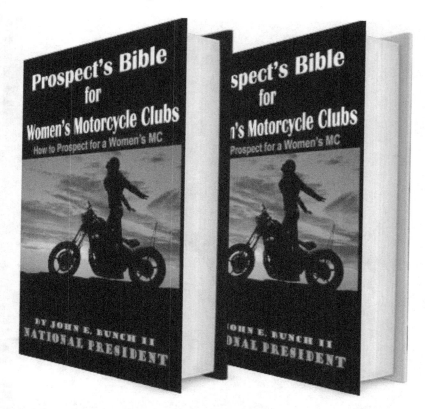

www.prospectsbibleforwomen.com

I have the ultimate faith in you! Be Sergeant-At-Arms! And take your MC to the next level!

Sincerely,

John E. Bunch II
Black Dragon
BSFFBS
A Breed Apart
Since 1974 and Still Strong.......///

Made in the USA
Middletown, DE
02 November 2023

41815274R00116